Project Delivery in Business-as-Usual Organizations

TIM CARROLL

Routledge
Taylor & Francis Group

LONDON AND NEW YORK

First published in paperback 2024

First published 2006 by Gower Publishing

Published 2016 by Routledge
4 Park Square, Milton Park, Abingdon, Oxon OX14 4RN

and by Routledge
605 Third Avenue, New York, NY 10158

Routledge is an imprint of the Taylor & Francis Group, an informa business

Publisher's Note
The publisher has gone to great lengths to ensure the quality of this reprint but points out that some imperfections in the original copies may be apparent.

British Library Cataloguing in Publication Data
Carroll, Tim
    Project delivery in business-as-usual organizations :
    making projects more valued in financial services
    1. Project management 2. Financial services industry –
    Management
    I. Title
    332.1'0684

Library of Congress Control Number: 2005931999

ISBN: 978-0-566-08629-8 (hbk)
ISBN: 978-1-03-283764-2 (pbk)
ISBN: 978-1-315-60237-0 (ebk)

DOI: 10.4324/9781315602370

Contents

List of Figures

List of Tables

CHAPTER 1

Introduction

This book tackles the challenges of delivering business projects in support of a company's strategic agenda. It is aimed at project and programme managers and those senior executives accountable for how project investments are managed. It is focused upon those companies where project delivery is not the primary aim of the organization – let's call them 'business-as-usual' companies.

BUSINESS-AS-USUAL COMPANIES?

We will discuss the nature of business-as-usual (BAU) companies more fully in Chapter 2. For now, let us consider them simply by contrasting with those companies where the delivery of projects is the prime, corporate aim. Those 'projectized' organizations include construction, IT systems integrators and aerospace in their numbers. Their success is based primarily upon the success of their projects, so project management is, not surprisingly, regarded as a core competency. The management of the company is focused around the success of the projects.

On a personal note, I spent my early career in such companies; one did not so much learn project management as absorb it from the very culture and fabric of the organization.

In the last decade, project management has progressed from these organizations into a very different type of organization; organizations whose primary purpose is the day-to-day BAU management of production, processing or sales activities. This definition includes most companies in financial services, where daily activity is focused upon processing financial transactions and managing customer relationships, but would also include many other organizations in varied industries.

If we think of a spectrum (100 per cent projectized at one end and 100 per cent BAU at the other) no single company could be classed as solely focused on project delivery and none could be classed as solely BAU, but it is clear that banks and, as an example, construction companies, exist in very different places along the spectrum.

Over the past decade these BAU organizations have adopted project management more widely as a discipline to better manage their investments in business change projects, a definition that includes the launch of new products, re-engineering of business processes and implementing new IT business systems.

Project management has moved into these areas for sound reasons. In today's volatile business world, the more effective delivery of change is seen as a key part of creating and maintaining strategic advantage, and project management offers a more disciplined, less risky way to deliver business change.

BUSINESS ISSUES TO BE ADDRESSED

Has this enthusiasm for project management delivered the improved performance that these organizations have sought? Most companies that have introduced project management to some degree would say that they have indeed gained improved results from applying project management disciplines and competencies to business change. They will rightly refer to their investments in methods, training and other disciplined approaches – the 'project improvement programmes' that are described in Chapter 3. I can testify, from personal experience, that these measures can improve the cost and time performance of projects by 15 to 20 per cent. They can also reduce the high failure rates on projects, much documented in surveys over the last decade, delivering more predictable results from projects.

Today, as we plan and manage business change projects better, using the disciplines of project and change management, is this enough? I observe a growing feeling in BAU organizations that project management has either not delivered its expectations or that, after a promising start, the rate of improvement has slowed. Here are some typical symptoms of this problem:

- Corporate improvement programmes for project management struggle to maintain executive support over the long term. In particular, the cost of maintaining specialist project management skills or centres of expertise is often difficult to support.

- It remains a challenge to implement specific project management techniques, in particular those that should operate at the more senior, politically sensitive levels of the company. Programme management and benefits management are cases in point and Chapter 4 presents some thoughts on both the successes and challenges of these techniques in BAU organizations.

- Project management disciplines are not used on all projects. In fact, it is often the most business-critical projects (which will attract the attention of the most senior executives) that do not use the disciplines of project management; projects to change corporate values, integrate acquisitions or change the corporate structure of the organization.

- Projects have not made the transition to being a valued part of normal business life. Despite their recognized contribution to delivering the company's strategic agenda, projects are still regarded as 'outside BAU' and the discipline of project management is still considered as some dark, technical specialism rather than a skill that solves business problems. This viewpoint leads to significant problems with how projects are sponsored and structured and how project staff are valued in the organization.

- The cost of project management is still regarded as an overhead or bureaucracy rather than an essential element of project delivery.

What do these symptoms tell us? Are these problems due to the unique nature of BAU organizations, when compared with projectized organizations? Are such organizations in some way naturally resistant to or inappropriate for the application of project management disciplines?

Perhaps project management has not travelled well from projectized to BAU organizations and the champions of project management's move into such organizations need to consider their cultures more deeply and adapt the approach so that the companies are more receptive to the disciplines.

If we agree that the implementation of improved project management practices is a project in itself and must be managed accordingly, perhaps the project management profession has broken its own principles about managing change; assessing the business context for the project and engaging stakeholders in language they comprehend?

RATIONALE FOR THIS BOOK

This is not a textbook on project management. It is assumed that the reader has some knowledge and experience of the subject, as a practitioner or a manager responsible for leading business change. Where I describe specific techniques it is because I believe that they will benefit from more straightforward, pragmatic descriptions than is usually the case. Hence they will be easier to describe and promote in BAU organizations.

The purpose of this book, having posed the questions above, is to consider why project delivery in BAU organizations must be addressed in a unique way. This subject is starting to receive public attention and some recent research has touched upon the cultural factors and perceptions in BAU organizations and their combined effect on the discipline of project management. However, most writings on project and programme management still treat all target organizations as similar (and as companies whose primary goal is the delivery of projects).

I would like this book to contribute to a wider debate about the way in which we apply project management in such organizations, so the first objective of this book is to offer practical advice on:

- how the techniques require some tailoring to reflect the unique character of BAU organizations;

- the change management approaches that can succeed when introducing project management to an organization;

I will then attempt to lead the reader to several conclusions during this book:

1. After showing good results in many BAU organizations, the discipline of project management must evolve if it is to continue delivering improved performance.

2. This evolution must recognize the differences between BAU and projectized organizations, to a greater extent than has been the case to date.

3. A key part of this changed approach is to build a competency of project delivery that is embedded within an organization, not positioned as a specialism.

4. A portfolio management approach is critical to the organization recognizing the strategic value of the capability to deliver projects successfully.

The title of this book refers to 'project delivery' not 'project management'. The distinction is intentional. It focuses on the business outcome, not the specialist skill. It signals also that if our discipline of project management is to be embedded in BAU life, we specialists must find subtler ways to promote it.

I have drawn from the financial services industry for much of my recent experience and have used that sector for most of the examples in this book. It is clear, though, from discussions with other companies, that the same issues exist in BAU organizations in many other industry sectors and I suggest that the same solutions will apply. As one example, the UK government sector currently has a clear focus on improving delivery performance across its change projects and this has resulted in much greater attention to the discipline of project management – to methodologies, training and the import of specialist assistance as parts of project improvement programmes. We can expect these measures to bear fruit in the short term but will the government sector, over time, suffer from the concerns now showing in those other sectors that moved into project management earlier, or will project management evolve to being regarded as a key element of project delivery, with sustained executive sponsorship for its improvement? I offer the opinion that adoption of the recommendations in this book will lead to a more positive outcome.

READING THIS BOOK

This book is constructed as a 'roadmap' (shown at the end of this chapter). It starts by considering the character of these BAU organizations and then progresses through the application of project, programme and portfolio management disciplines. Each chapter produces, I hope, a tangible outcome for the reader.

There is a linkage from each chapter to the next and the chapters progressively establish a business context for project management. However, the chapters can stand alone and so can be read in any order.

Each individual chapter of this book is also presented as a roadmap that describes the drivers for a disciplined approach or project management technique, then describes the approach at a summary level and concludes with practical advice on implementing the approach in a BAU organization. In other words, each chapter is described as a project life cycle that takes the reader from business need, through a solution and on to practical implementation.

SO, WHAT ARE THE BENEFITS OF READING THIS BOOK?

As project management professionals, we must take our own medicine. You should be clear, as you would want to be for any project investment, that there is a range of tangible benefits as a return on investment for the time expended in reading this book. I suggest the following:

1. The consideration of how a framework of project management approaches can be tailored and applied in practice in BAU organizations (Chapter 3) offers tangible benefits in improved project performance for BAU organizations that are in the earlier stages of improving project performance.

2. The hypothesis (again in Chapter 3) that many BAU organizations would be better served by building an embedded capability for delivering strategic change in addition to building a specialist project management competency is perhaps controversial to professional project managers, but one that I offer as a means to re-energize project improvement programmes that are losing momentum and to obtain long-term corporate support for the competency.

3. In Chapter 4, the cautionary notes about the use of programme management can avoid wasted effort and a loss of executive support for these disciplines. They can help to embed the key (and often unloved!) discipline of benefits management into the organization.

4. Portfolio management seeks to maximize the strategic benefit that the company reaps from its investment in change projects. Recently many BAU companies have been exploring these techniques as a response to the increasing change and volatility in their business environment. With such attention comes market hype and complexity, but little practical advice, so Chapter 5 offers some views on the practical application of these valuable techniques.

5. In this book's conclusion in Chapter 6, I bring together the concepts of portfolio management (embedding projects in their rightful place within the organization's strategic agenda) and the embedded skill of delivering change, to promote an approach where projects can make the transition from 'outside BAU' to being 'a part of BAU'. This combination of embedded approaches can improve the direct benefits of change projects, but also offers a way of articulating as never before how projects support the strategic agenda – of how the projects really are inside BAU, a part of BAU. This in turn will lead to greater, top-down executive support for efforts to improve the capability

and maturity of project delivery, support that has traditionally been hard to maintain.

With a portfolio approach finally pushing change projects onto the chief executive's desk and demonstrating clearly how the collected projects deliver key parts of the strategic agenda, supplemented by considering project delivery as an embedded skill rather than project management as a specialist skill, I believe that we have an approach that can create sustained executive support, ensuring:

- better recognition of the corporate value of the skill of delivering business change projects;

- improved performance in applying that skill in BAU organizations.

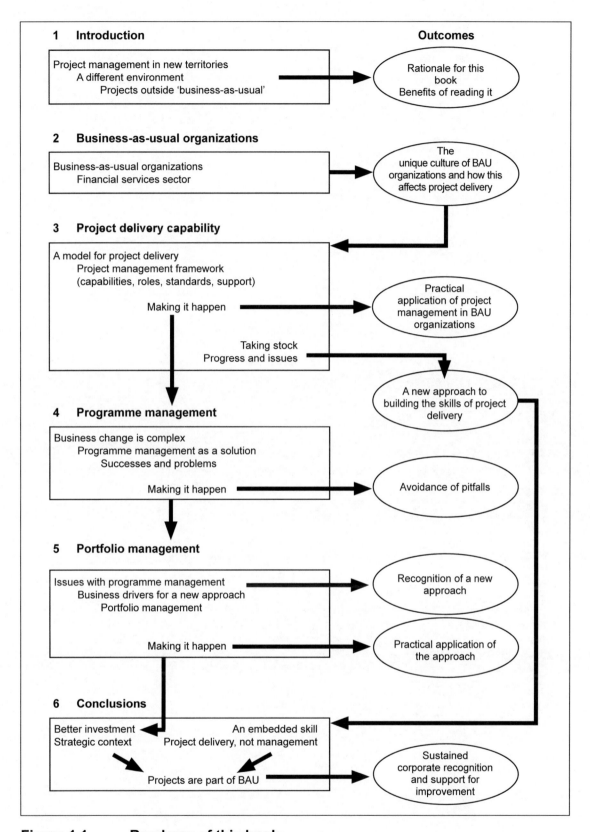

Figure 1.1   Roadmap of this book

Business-as-Usual Organizations

ROADMAP FOR CHAPTER 2

This chapter introduces business-as-usual organizations, contrasting them with projectized companies (in areas such as construction). While some of the different challenges in delivering projects in BAU organizations can be attributed to the 'soft' nature of business change projects, it is proposed that there are distinct, cultural differences that are more important to consider.

The banking sector is highlighted to demonstrate that these differences also apply at an industry level, to reflect particular cultural factors and behaviours in each industry.

The chapter concludes with three propositions that underpin the rest of this book. A hypothetical example will hopefully convince the reader that these propositions are probable and worthwhile of further consideration!

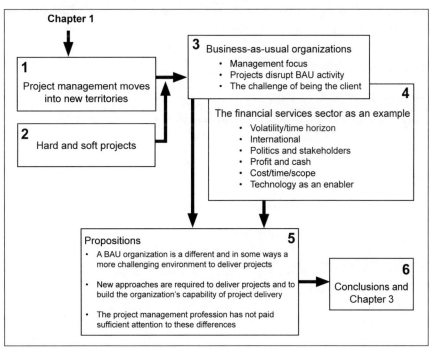

Roadmap for Chapter 2

1 PROJECT MANAGEMENT MOVES INTO NEW TERRITORIES

Project management grew as a discipline in companies involved in capital projects where the delivery of projects was the prime, corporate aim. They are 'project management companies'.

Other companies that have been in the forefront of project management did not have projects as their sole, corporate aim, but they recognized early on that their business depended fundamentally on the ability to deliver new products to market in a timely and effective manner. Defence agencies were early enthusiasts, particularly in the USA where project management disciplines and techniques were shaped on critical defence projects in the 1960s and 1970s. Pharmaceutical companies also adopted project management techniques to provide discipline on drug developments, where timescales are long and each project is a speculative venture requiring a major proportion of the company's resources.

Consultancy organizations and IT solution integrators recognized the value of the disciplines in the 1980s and 1990s to manage the delivery of their solutions and related tasks such as re-engineering business processes.

In the last two decades, project management has progressed from these organizations into a very different type of organization; organizations whose primary purpose is the day-to-day BAU management of production, processing or sales activities.

While some of these organizations have long used project management disciplines within specialist areas (product launches, premises as examples), over the past decade they have generally adopted project management as a core discipline to better manage their investments in business change projects:

- re-engineering business processes
- internal reorganizations
- transferring work to outsource partners
- integrating acquisitions
- driving cultural change
- changing brand identity
- responding to new regulations
- improving IT systems and infrastructure
- improving how customer relationships are managed.

The volatility in today's business world is increasing this demand for discipline in managing business change, as executives know that the world will change around them and any shortcomings in delivering change projects are likely to reduce the desired benefits arising from such investments.

For example, in the 1980s and 1990s there were many studies on the business aspects of corporate mergers and acquisitions. Most have focused upon the strategy and business drivers for the merger or acquisition and whether the desired benefits (synergies, costs, revenues) have been realized. More recently, the focus has shifted somewhat to look at the approaches that lead to success during the implementation of the acquisition – how it is integrated into the acquiring organization in such a way that it delivers benefits on a sustainable basis. The benefits of clear goals, good planning, disciplined control of progress and careful attention to managing the affected staff (all classical components of a change project) have been correlated with improved benefits and the creation of greater shareholder value.

This move of project management into business change is reflected in the focus of the project management profession (see Figure 2.1). Project management techniques evolved as a means of managing complexity. Critical path networking and then more integrated project control systems looked for the balanced management of cost, time and scope. The concept of a project life cycle gave structure to projects, and key processes for managing a project were defined. The focus of this project management competency was very much on the delivery of a solution – some tangible deliverables such as a new bridge, road, or petrochemical facility. As project management moved into the field of business change the solutions were still described in terms of their tangible deliverables – IT systems, process models or new products.

In addition to the technical aspects of project management (the science of project management, as it was often termed) the project management profession paid increased attention to the skills and behaviours required to motivate and lead teams on the delivery of projects. The various organization structures that could be used to deliver projects were the subject of research, as were the personal skills and attributes of those who lead projects. We often called this the art of managing projects.

As project management started to make inroads to projects that deliver information technology or to re-engineer internal business processes, this focus on the people aspects of project management evolved to address the challenge of managing change – the less tangible deliverables of the project. We recognized that these types of projects needed attention to the involvement of affected staff and to clear communication of the goals, or staff would not be supportive of the endeavour.

The project management profession realized that it must widen its definition of the scope of the project beyond the delivery of a 'solution'. The delivery of the project's tangible deliverables (such as some new technology or redesigned process) is only a part of the whole project process. The concepts of programme management and benefits management have gained in prominence to address these broader implications of change, including the realization of the benefits that the organization sought in return for the project investment.

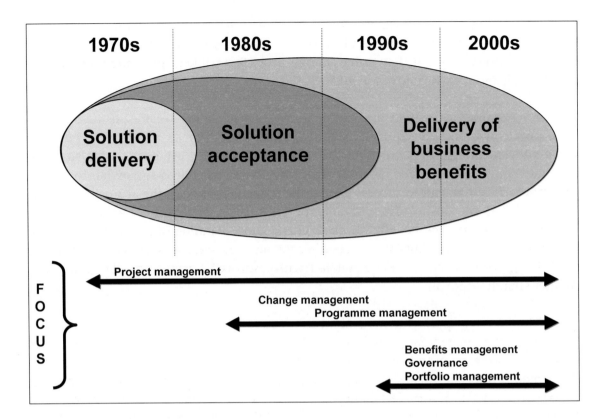

Figure 2.1   The evolution of project management

In the early stages of this attention to the organization-wide value of project management, the term 'management by projects' was coined. It was the first indication that the sum of projects in an organization might equate to its agenda for change and growth. This was a concept that has now become more applicable in practice through the development of programme management and portfolio management.

In recent years, this focus on engagement of the business has broadened. There is an increased emphasis on the right sponsorship and governance that will provide not only the support of individual staff whose working life is directly affected by the project but also broader, corporate support for the project so that it can deliver its objectives despite a changing business environment and competing priorities.

This growth in the use of project management for business change has led to greater prominence of the discipline and this has been mirrored by the entry of project management into the curricula of business schools.

What is so special about delivering projects in this new territory of BAU managing change in organizations? Is it merely the type of project that is typically undertaken or is it a wider, cultural difference from projectized organizations? Let's look first at the types of projects.

2 HARD AND SOFT PROJECTS

We often call projects either 'hard' or 'soft'. Definitions of hard and soft vary, but hard projects are typically based on solid, scientifically defined objectives where there is limited scope for interpretation (building a road, for example, where the final deliverable can be clearly measured against its planned scope and specification). Soft projects might have less tangible goals or might have outcomes that are more oriented to people, open to interpretation or subject to differing expectations by stakeholders (embedding a set of corporate values across an organization being an extreme example).

It is generally accepted that considering projects in varying degrees of hard or soft is a useful aid to establishing the right project approach, the required skills of the project team, the management methods adopted and how much of the team's effort is applied to the technical or human aspects of the project.

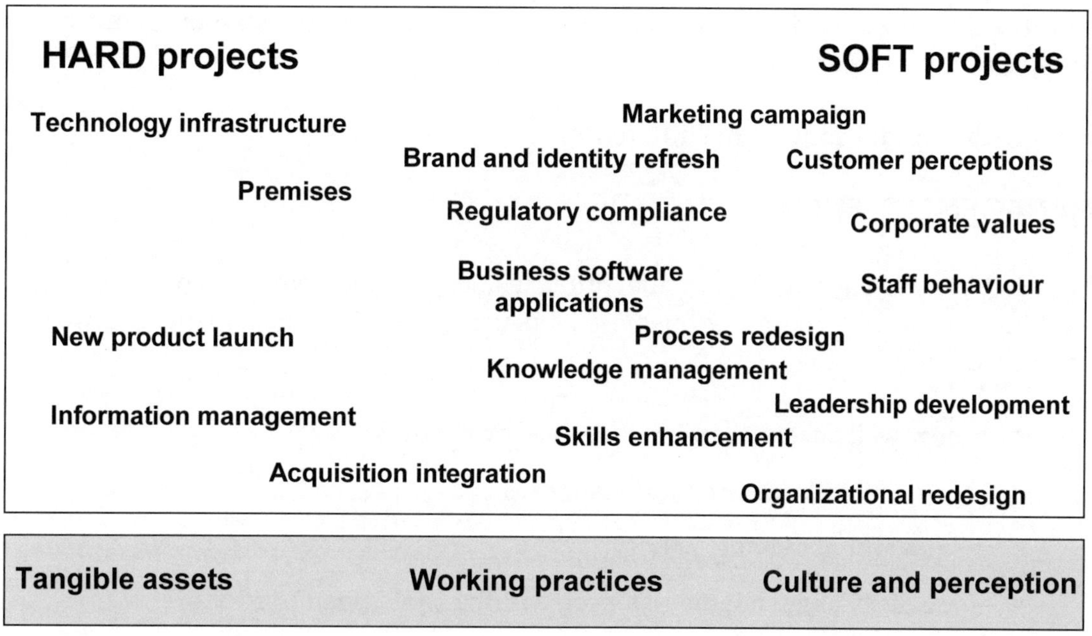

HARD projects

Technology infrastructure

Premises

New product launch

Information management

Acquisition integration

SOFT projects

Marketing campaign

Brand and identity refresh   Customer perceptions

Regulatory compliance

Corporate values

Business software   Staff behaviour
applications

Process redesign

Knowledge management

Leadership development

Skills enhancement

Organizational redesign

Tangible assets   Working practices   Culture and perception

Figure 2.2   Hard and soft projects

As Figure 2.2 shows, there is a spectrum of hardness and softness and most projects are a blend of both. On the face of it, a move of an organization to new office premises is a hard project, with building selection, construction and fit-out being key elements of the project. The contractors working on the project will see their scope of work as a hard project. However, anyone who has worked on such a project from within the owner's organization will be keenly aware of the softer aspects, such as where the building should be located to suit employees' preferences, how space will be allocated in the new office, what style of interior space will be best. All of these discussions involve many stakeholders, office politics and differing points of view. Eventually, while the goal of the new office will include hard outcomes such as cost reductions, it will also include softer outcomes such as teams working more closely together. If the staff are not happy in their new facility (a very soft measure!) then the project will have failed.

The implementation of IT systems is a similar blend of hard and soft aspects, where the specification is open to interpretation and the right engagement and perceptions of stakeholders are critical to overall project success.

3 BUSINESS-AS-USUAL ORGANIZATIONS

It is tempting to consider the use of project management in its traditional (engineering) and new (business change) applications as simply the difference between hard and soft projects.

While this distinction is certainly part of the issue, there is a more fundamental and critical point to consider. This is that these business change projects are taking place in organizations whose primary aim is not the delivery of projects. The culture of such organizations is shaped by everyday business activity, not the delivery of projects, and this difference fundamentally affects the way in which project management, as a discipline, must be carried out.

Let's consider some of the differences.

MANAGEMENT FOCUS

In organizations such as banks, the primary focus of the senior management each working day is the conduct of business as usual. A bank's management team will be concerned with:

- how well customer transactions are proceeding;
- competitive pressures and responses;
- sales and marketing activity;
- regularly assessing the risk profile of the bank's loan portfolio;
- managing the cost base;
- motivating and leading staff;
- ensuring compliance with expected practices and regulations.

Of course the senior management will also be considering how to grow the organization and how to make significant changes in the business portfolio and efficiency of operations. They will be spending time steering such endeavours. At the more senior levels of management an increased proportion of time will be spent on the future of the organization rather than its present-day operations. The majority of management time, though, will be spent on directing BAU activity, and rightly so. For a UK plc, the martketplace measures the success of the company twice a year through its annual and interim results and the management team will lose the confidence of the marketplace if short-term progress is unsatisfactory.

Projects are relatively long-term endeavours (perhaps a typical implementation timescale is six months to a year, with a further one or two years until the project breaks even and starts to generate profit). So projects will always come lower down the corporate agenda (and the executive's diary management) than myriad BAU activities.

There is also an argument (which I accept will vary by industry) that in some cases the cost of project investments is actually less worthy of management attention than BAU activity. In a bank, for example, the difference between good and bad performance on the bad debts from the loan portfolio is likely to be an order of magnitude larger than the difference between good and bad performance in managing project costs. Where would you spend your time and energy as you drive your team towards year-end performance targets?

So we can argue that such companies are right to be spending their time primarily on managing BAU activity.

To make matters worse for a champion of project management, we should reflect that most senior managers of such organizations have not participated frequently in the conduct of business projects. During their career they might have directly led a project, but it is more likely that they will have participated in projects less directly as line managers, either being in some way accountable for a project or being affected by the results of the project. They are not likely to be receptive to a set of new techniques and practices if they have little empathy with the trials and tribulations of project teams.

In summary, this is a difficult point at which to start a campaign to improve project management in such an organization! It is also a shock, and I speak from personal experience here: despite the project management profession's views of the importance of projects to an organization's development and the undeniable logic that the portfolio of business change projects helps drive the organization's strategic change agenda, the reality is that project delivery comes some way down the daily agenda of such organizations.

PROJECTS DISRUPT BAU ACTIVITY

This ambivalence to projects would be a challenge in itself. The situation worsens, though, for any champion of project management in such organizations, for projects actually disrupt current BAU activity. Any change project needs a core team to drive activity and needs varied involvement from subject matter experts and line managers who will be affected by the project. This business input is critical, as we see in the post mortems of the many IT-based projects where the lack of sufficient user involvement is a common source of project failures.

Allocating the time of internal staff to a project causes tensions:

- The business has to reorganize its resources to address both the project and BAU. Using short-term, external resource to provide business expertise to the project rarely works well because of the lack of ongoing ownership, so the usual approach is to second internal staff to the project and backfill them with temporary staff on BAU work. This transition must be carefully managed if the quality of BAU work is not to suffer.

- These project secondments also cause concerns on a personal level. They take the staff away from their place in the internal hierarchy, which is an uncomfortable experience, and place them into a project process of which they might have little prior experience. If not carefully managed, the re-integration of the staff back into BAU activity after the project can also lead to staff dissatisfaction.

These issues can lead to projects being discussed in quite negative terms, as diversions from BAU, as assignments that are personally unattractive, as 'outside BAU'.

(I carried out a benchmarking exercise recently with 11 banks. The banks varied in their project management maturity and in how enthusiastically they had adopted project management as a discipline, but there was an almost universal view that, despite the organization recognizing that projects were important to the business and investing in project management practices, the projects were considered as being 'outside BAU'. This is a long way from our profession's view that the projects are an integral part of how the business grows and manages its affairs.)

If a project impedes upon and disrupts BAU activity, then the role of a project manager is also likely to impede upon the area of responsibility of line managers affected by the project. Even if the efforts of the project manager are intended to be constructive, there will be sensitive areas, particularly when the business case, stakeholder management or the honest portrayal of project risks are involved. This can have a negative impact on how the project manager and the discipline of project management are perceived.

THE CHALLENGE OF BEING THE CLIENT

In traditional areas of project management, such as construction, the client or owner of the delivered project solution is often (but I accept not always) experienced in acting in that capacity. The client knows the life cycle that a project follows and appreciates the issues that arise during the life cycle. But BAU organizations spend most of their time on BAU activity, so when a project arises it is likely that they are either inexperienced in acting as the client or find it difficult to access whatever knowledge they have gained from projects in other parts of the organization.

As Figure 2.3 shows, the client's life cycle for the project is long (longer than the implementation process upon which project managers typically focus) and includes a number of politically-sensitive responsibilities, from gathering support for the project in its early stages through to realizing business benefits. These broader aspects of project delivery are still challenging to those in the project management profession who spend their working lives on projects (as examples, benefits realization is still difficult to achieve in practice and whether the project manager should have responsibility for the business case is still debated in publications). If these areas are challenging for the project management professionals then I would argue that it is not surprising that anyone who is involved only occasionally on projects will find them very daunting.

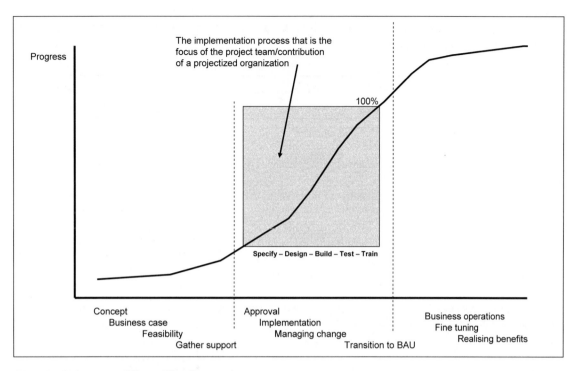

Figure 2.3   The client's project scope

As it is focused upon BAU activity, the organization is also poorly equipped with systems and processes that would help the management of projects. Most BAU companies have limited capability in project control tools or in project accounting (either as a concept or in the form of suitable accounting systems.)

Another aspect of being a BAU-focused client is that the organization has a structure and hierarchy that is tailored to the BAU needs of the organization. Whereas projectized organizations have developed organizational models that particularly suit the needs of project delivery, these are difficult to create in BAU organizations. For example, many BAU organizations have limited experience in acting in a matrix fashion, where the organization aligns itself to both functions (for consistent technical standards and quality) and projects (for focus and clear objectives).

It is often very difficult for the project to gain the right attention from affected functions when the existing organizational hierarchy is so much stronger than the project structure (which is of course temporary in nature). Sometimes this strength of the existing structure, together with political considerations, can overpower the project, resulting in decisions being driven by BAU managers who do not have the requisite skills or whose agenda is not the same as that required for the success of the project.

See Table 2.1 for a summary of the differences in the delivery of projects between projectized organizations and BAU organizations implementing business change.

Table 2.1   **Contrasting the delivery of projects in projectized and BAU organizations**

	Projectized	*Business change in a BAU organization*
Primary focus of the organization and organizational design	Project delivery	BAU service delivery
Typical project	Hard with soft areas	Soft with hard areas
Business case	Limited to profitability of delivering a solution Subject to risks in solution delivery	Depends on broader engagement within the organization Subject to risks in the business environment
Staff affected	Localized, dedicated	Includes dispersed, part-time contributors
Short-term profitability of the organisation is impacted by...	Project management efficiency	BAU business performance
Experience of senior management	Project-based	BAU-based
Learning from previous projects	Institutionalized	Limited
Perceptions/attitudes	'Our business is the sum of our projects' 'Projects are our BAU'	'Projects are outside BAU' 'Projects disrupt BAU'

The Scottish Parliament construction project was completed in 2004 (significantly late and over budget) and has been the subject of much press comment and a published governmental report. We can consider this as an example of a project delivered by a BAU organization, for while governments deliver many projects they are primarily BAU in nature. Although a full analysis of the project is outside the scope of this book, the published report highlights a number of the features that have been discussed above, including unrealistic expectations, poor organizational structures and control processes, together with inadequate project delivery skills of BAU line managers (see the panel on the next page).

4 THE FINANCIAL SERVICES SECTOR AS AN EXAMPLE

The descriptions above of BAU organizations will apply to many different industry sectors and I believe that the lessons and approaches in this book are relevant to many sectors. However, each sector and company also brings a unique culture that reflects its needs and history and this culture must also be recognized when applying the disciplines of project management. We can use as an example the financial services sector and banking in particular, considering some cultural factors and behaviours that can appear on business change projects.

Scottish Parliament

The project has been criticized for its procurement method, the management structures put in place to deliver it and the lack of adequate budgeting or cost controls for what was described as a uniquely complex building.

The choice in 1998 by Scottish Office civil servants of a 'construction management' procurement vehicle to deliver the building was made under considerable pressure from political sponsors to build the parliament fast.

Officials chose this route because it allowed work on the building to begin before its design was finalized. The alternative of hiring a lead contractor to build to a fixed price was deemed too slow for a completion date originally set for July 2001. But construction management was a vehicle unsuited for most public sector building projects. This was because it left most of the risk with the client rather than contractors and required considerable construction industry expertise to manage – mostly absent among the project's civil servant (BAU) managers.

The complex project required a single point of leadership but responsibility was instead divided among several parties, including both officials and politicians.

There was no attempt to set a cost ceiling and the official report concluded that it was not clear how important cost was compared with time and quality.

VOLATILITY/TIME HORIZON

These organizations exist in a volatile environment. Some functions, such as trading, are extremely volatile and this leads to a short-term view and short planning horizons. It is very difficult for a project team to engage users as it is difficult for a long-term project to compete with immediate BAU demands from the trading floor (in contrast, insurance and pension companies tend to have a longer-term view, consistent with their organizational focus).

INTERNATIONAL

Many financial services organizations are also international, so any projects that are strategically important are likely to have global application. There is a perennial balancing act to be achieved between global standardization and localized business needs as each country operation will also have its own views on how the project should be conducted. This provides an extreme example of the challenges of managing stakeholders. This international dimension makes projects extremely challenging and has implications for the level of skill required, the tools and techniques used to conduct the project and how communications are managed.

POLITICS AND STAKEHOLDERS

As a generalization, banks are relatively political organizations with strong, established hierarchies and a performance culture that results in a significant proportion of a manager's income arising from performance bonuses. Where an organization's structure is also relatively federal rather than centralist (often the case in banks) and the project team has to engage varied parts of the organization in the project, this will dictate the styles of leadership and communication that the project team must employ. Attending to stakeholders (both supporters and opponents of the project) is critical to project success. Engaging affected staff becomes a key challenge.

PROFIT AND CASH

All companies, in any sector, have to manage business performance through the profit and loss account, cash flow and the balance sheet. Projects affect all three:

- cash costs for the investment cost of the project;

- immediate impacts on the profit and loss account (where the project's cash costs cannot be capitalized);

- the eventual impact of the capitalized costs on the balance sheet and profit and loss account;

- the eventual benefits from the project, in both cash and profit terms.

When compared with other sectors, banks have huge balance sheets. This is because their assets and liabilities include sizeable loans made to customers and funding received as customer deposits; the much smaller fees and interest charges drive the profit and loss account. So, balance sheet considerations drive projects much less than in other sectors.

Cash is readily available and acquired at relatively low cost, but in contrast the marketplace pays very close attention to the profit and loss performance of the banks and to their cost/income ratios (operating costs as a proportion of income). This attention to the profit and loss account rather than cash or balance sheet leads to interesting dynamics in the management of business projects:

- A tendency for project timescales to be adjusted to minimize the impact on the current profit and loss accounting period. An example would be the delay of a go-live date into the next period, when the capitalization of costs will also be deferred. The risk when making such changes is that the impact on the overall business case for the project is not properly considered. In addition, the impact of any delay or slow-down upon the cost of the project is also ignored or under-estimated.

- The annual window that is used for setting business targets and cost budgets also leads to 'annual projects'. These start in January (or whatever month represents the start of the new financial year and the availability of new funds) and they typically and conveniently are estimated as taking 12 months to deliver (usually an estimate based on hope rather than fact). Of course, some projects will take longer than a year to deliver, in which case the project merely seeks a new budget in the next financial period to complete the project. The danger is that the organization loses sight of the overall cost and business case of the project, merely seeing a series of annual slices of the project. These annual projects run a serious risk of not being run as projects with a defined goal, but as BAU departments.

- The flow of cash through the project is a measure of the work being undertaken. It results from the costs of the project team and external purchases. The profile of cash spend over time obviously varies from the profit and loss profile where costs are capitalized as assets on the balance sheet. One issue for banks is that their focus on profit and loss measures tends to give misleading information as to how far the project has progressed towards completion.

COST/TIME/SCOPE

The above analysis does not imply that financial services organizations do not manage their costs, just that their culture and business environment force particular behaviours onto project teams. In fact, financial services organizations pay great attention to managing costs – for managing money is what they do for a living. If we consider the project manager's three objectives for managing cost, time and scope/quality (the classical project management triangle of objectives), there is a tendency for banks to manage the costs very tightly but to allow both time and scope to flex. If this is done informally then there are risks to the overall business case (for if the delivered scope is reduced this might have a significant impact upon the flow of benefits that is not always appreciated by the project team).

Such informal reductions in scope can cause great problems in multi-country roll-outs of new systems and processes. In the team's rush to achieve the launch in the pilot location, some short cuts are taken, some functionality might be sacrificed and some tasks will be done superficially. It is easy to fall into this trap on business change projects – reducing the effort on communications or training might have limited initial downside on the pilot site and will attract little attention (while not completing the last span of a road bridge tends to attract attention!). However, when the project team moves on to other locations, the exclusions start to cause real problems:

- Temporary fixes or short-cuts impede roll-out activity and require remedial work.

- Multiple versions of the solution to cater for remedial work create complexity and extra costs.

- Poor change management is the result when the project team cannot give the same undivided attention to multiple sites as it gave to the pilot site.

Once the pilot phase has gone live (much publicized, no doubt), the organization has a tendency to assume that the hard work has been completed and the rest of the roll-out will be quite simple. It comes as a shock when the project team returns to request more funds to address the increased complexity of the roll-out and this in turn often results in a slow-down of the roll-out to reduce the short-term cost impact. This increases total project costs and might defer the delivery of the full, steady-state benefits from the project.

TECHNOLOGY AS AN ENABLER

Banking operations are underpinned by information technology. Of course this is true for BAU organizations in all sectors, but particularly so for banking where there is no physical product and where a huge number of transactions occurs daily. Hence, much of the project workload is made up of IT resources, software, hardware and communications networks. Business change projects might have 50 to 80 per cent of their costs allocated to IT work, with the balance being on process re-engineering, change management and project management. The IT work can overshadow the other elements of the project (which are just as important to project success) and can even overshadow the business rationale for projects. The danger signs are that one hears people in banks talking about 'IT projects' or of particular projects as being 'owned by Technology'. These perceptions dilute the business ownership of projects and focus the attention on technology deliverables (just a part of the project solution) rather than the business case (the project outcome).

In conclusion, these observations about the financial services sector serve to demonstrate that different industries will exhibit unique cultures and issues, which will affect the risks of projects and the behaviours of project teams as well as influencing the maturity of project management practices. We could draw up a similar analysis for other sectors, for example the government sector where our analysis would highlight characteristics including:

- the huge size and implementation complexity of infrastructure changes, which result in very lengthy timescales;

- the influence of changes in policy as governments react to priorities and public opinion;

- how making policy is still regarded as more career-enhancing than the delivery of solutions;

- political desires for sharing funding with private enterprise, leading to very complex commercial and risk-sharing models for project delivery;

- the impact of public-sector funding approaches;

- politicians' desires for 'quick wins' and the impression of immediate action.

5 PROPOSITIONS

There are three key assertions in this book.

First is that most business change projects in industry today are taking place in organizations whose primary aim is not the delivery of projects and that these organizations provide a different and in some ways more challenging environment within which to deliver projects than is provided by a projectized business.

Second is that because the culture of such organizations is shaped by everyday business activity, not the delivery of projects, different approaches are required to deliver projects and to engage the organization in building a generic project management capability. These approaches must include demonstrating the business context for projects across the organization.

These views have been shaped by personal experience. I have delivered projects in both projectized and BAU organizations and built the project management capabilities in both types of organization. The differences between projectized and BAU organizations have become more evident during these experiences. What has also become evident, and is my third assertion, is that our project management profession has not paid sufficient attention to the unique nature of BAU organizations when attempting to migrate traditional project management approaches.

This is not an area that has received much structured research, so there is no scientific evidence at hand. Let's adopt the next best approach and use a hypothesis to test out these views.

Let's take a construction management company, a projectized organization where managing engineering projects is the prime goal of the organization, and now consider how it delivers an unusual project – a project that delivers to the organization itself rather than to a client. An example would be the implementation of a new system for accounting and financial control. If my assertions are correct, then we could assume that:

- The construction company will be more successful than a BAU organization in implementing the technical core of the system (software, IT infrastructure). This is because the construction company is more attuned to the life cycle and issues of project delivery. There will be a clearer focus on the initial planning stage of the project than in a BAU organization and project risks will be considered more carefully.

- The construction company will still find it difficult to clearly define all the requirements of the new system (a softer project issue).

- The construction company will also find the broader aspects of the implementation difficult (re-engineering processes, engaging staff from all departments in ensuring the success of the project, training staff).

- Staff will complain that the project is distracting them from their primary daily business activity (which in this case is managing construction projects).

- It will also be hard to get an internal candidate to run this important project as it takes them away from BAU activity and the added value to their careers is not clear. So leadership might be given to external parties and this will lead to other tensions on the project and issues related to transition of the new system into operations.

- Sponsorship will be strong within the Finance function but the construction management function will delegate ownership to fairly junior staff that can be spared from ('more pressing') BAU activity. This will lead to delays in escalating and resolving issues.

Does this hypothesis ring true? I suggest that it does and shows that the construction company will:

- be more attuned to the project process than a BAU organization, which will improve its chances of success in delivering the new system;

- have more inherent capability than a BAU organization to manage such a project…

but will still suffer from a number of issues, only some of which reflect the soft nature of the project; others reflect the unusual nature of the project when compared with BAU activity in the organization.

(One can sometimes see the same issues when a software company tries to implement its own business software applications within its own organization. While the company is well attuned to delivering solutions to customers, in which case the customer usually undertakes most of the change management, applying the software to itself is difficult and the change management challenges are considerable.)

6 CONCLUSIONS

BAU organizations are different to projectized organizations and offer unique challenges when delivering projects. Since they are also the focus of much of the project management profession today, they are deserving of closer analysis, but to date they have received limited research attention other than work on the nature of soft change projects. As I have described above, BAU organizations offer a range of challenges, many of which are due to their corporate culture, not the character of the project. The rest of this book outlines how we can improve project delivery in BAU organizations by:

- building the project delivery capability of the organization and tailoring project management disciplines to reflect the culture of BAU organizations (Chapter 3);

- aligning projects more closely with the strategic agenda of the organization through the use of programmes and addressing some of the issues that impede the implementation of programme management in BAU organizations (see Chapter 4);

- implementing portfolio management to improve this alignment and the effectiveness of project investments (Chapter 5);

- using these approaches to demonstrate both the business context for projects and their contribution to the organization's agenda of strategic change, leading to an organization that is more supportive of project delivery as a valued business capability (Chapter 6).

Building the Organization's Project Delivery Capability

ROADMAP FOR CHAPTER 3

Chapters 1 and 2 have described project delivery in BAU organizations. Chapter 3 will now focus upon the techniques that can be used to improve the organization's capability to staff, organize and deliver projects on a regular basis. This chapter will consider the key issues that must be addressed to deliver business change projects successfully and then propose a 'project management framework' – a framework of measures that helps an organization to acquire project delivery skills at both individual and organizational levels.

Many companies have invested in such frameworks in recent years. They have delivered improvements in project success rates and have made project management into a more valued and recognized role within BAU organizations. However, these frameworks must be introduced sensitively, recognizing the culture of the organization, or they will lose momentum; this chapter proposes some ways of making each part of the framework acceptable in BAU organizations.

In recent years, the focus of these frameworks has been primarily on the development of a specialist skill within the organization. This chapter concludes with a proposition: to generate sustainable project success, a BAU company must also embed the skill of managing change deeply into its organization and corporate competencies. This proposition has significant implications for how companies develop skills and organize project teams and this chapter describes how this embedded approach will change the design of a project management framework.

This chapter's conclusion poses a question – does the project management profession have to adopt a more subtle (perhaps humble) approach in order to continue improving how change projects are delivered in BAU organizations?

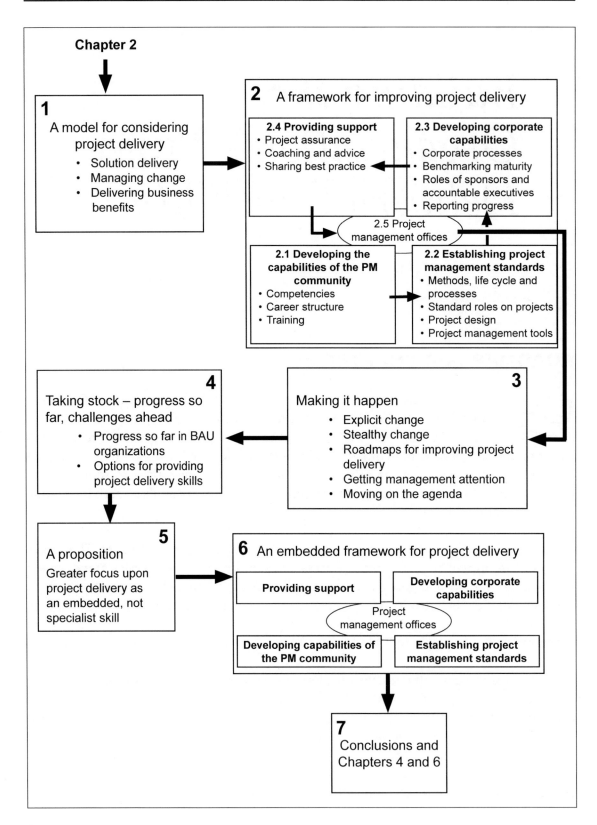

Roadmap for Chapter 3

1 A MODEL FOR CONSIDERING PROJECT DELIVERY

In most companies, the success rate of business change projects is low. In this book I will not attempt to reference the many industry studies and surveys of the topic. However, I will offer the following overview of how projects proceed and how they succeed or fail.

First, we can consider, simplistically, any change project as having four steps within its life cycle (see Figure 3.1):

- an opportunity or problem to be addressed;
- the design and delivery of a solution;
- the adoption and use of the solution by the business;
- the delivery of business benefits.

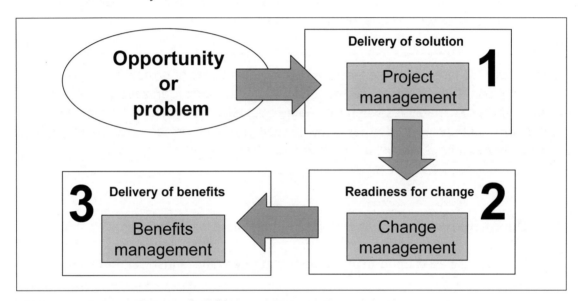

Figure 3.1   Three areas of potential failure

A change project is the process of taking an organization from some present state to some desired future state. This takes us through a period of transition, a period which is unstable and risky.

The first step is that we identify that we have a problem to face or have an opportunity that we can take advantage of in our business life. To take advantage of that opportunity or to fix that problem we need to deliver a number of things; let's call those things the project's 'solutions'. They could be new processes or ways of working, they could be about training and improving the skills of our staff, investing in new capital equipment or (as is frequent for most businesses today) investing in new information technology solutions.

We need our organization to be prepared to receive the solutions, so that they are properly and enthusiastically implemented and therefore lead to the effective business use of the solution.

We are only investing in these projects in order to produce a number of business benefits, which could be financial or non-financial. In the financial area we would have benefits like improved revenues, reductions in costs in areas like staff or materials, higher quality resulting in fewer processing errors, lower staff turnover or the elimination of activities to reduce costs. The benefits can also be described in non-financial terms, for example as better customer service or greater corporate flexibility so that the company can react faster to future changes in the market.

Each of these three areas is addressed through some specialist techniques:

- project management concerned with the delivery of the solution;

- change management concerned with the acceptance and use of the solution by our people;

- benefits management concerned with ensuring that the desired business benefits really do flow from the project.

As we will see later, all three disciplines are really a part of project management, but let's use these different terms for now. Does your organization consider all three of these capabilities when managing business change? Don't be concerned with terminology and whether they are all parts of project management or separate disciplines; focus on whether they are all in place!

There have been many surveys and industry statistics of how projects perform in each of these three stages of the project life cycle. I offer the following analysis as a 'poll of polls' which is based upon many industry surveys. The statistics are not claimed to be definitive or highly accurate but they summarize the trends evident in the various surveys and provide a means to consider the issues of project delivery and then construct approaches that will improve the rate of success.

We start with a hundred change projects that companies initiate (see Figure 3.2). The general industry view is that perhaps 40 per cent of them fail in that they never even get to the stage of completing their solutions (their new IT investment, their new ways of working, and so on). Typically these 40 per cent of projects get cancelled or reach the delivery stage but are so seriously flawed that they are never going to result in any significant business benefits.

Out of the 60 projects that do deliver their solutions, about 60 per cent (say 35) are fully implemented by the business. That means that the business users of the solution do not accept it enthusiastically in about 40 per cent of cases; during the project we have failed to involve our people such that they would truly use the solution for the benefit of the business.

Now we have about 35 of the 100 projects that are going to be accepted and properly placed into business operation. But our problems don't stop there, because most surveys these days will show that only about 20 per cent of change projects actually deliver the business benefits that they have originally promised, which means another 15 or about 40 per cent of the accepted solutions do not deliver the expected business benefits.

So only 20 per cent of our projects end up producing the benefits we desired and at each of the three stages (solution delivery, readiness for change and benefits delivery) we had project failures. Our failure rate was something like 40 per cent at each stage of the life cycle – the message being that failures are quite evenly spread across the three stages.

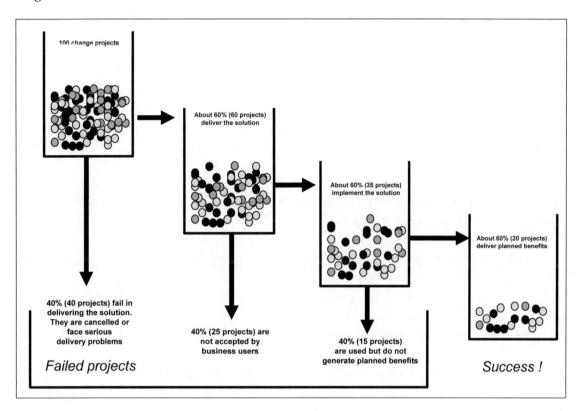

Figure 3.2   A 'poll of polls' on project failure

We can look now at the reasons for failure and what we can do to improve our success at each stage.

SOLUTION DELIVERY

Considering first the fact that complete solutions are not delivered, here we are in the area of project management techniques. Why is it that we cannot build some of the things that we set out to do? The reasons often relate to poor discipline, for example in poor definition of requirements or poor planning. Often there are unrealistic expectations because of poor plans, and that means we underestimate the complexity of projects, so they end up taking far longer or cost far more than we anticipated. Poor discipline can also hurt projects in areas such as change control where scope changes are allowed to affect the conduct of the project.

Without discipline in the planning and conduct of the project, success rates suffer. Surveys typically show that anything to do with technology or the actual technical content of the projects features very low down in the areas of failure. Most of the emphasis is about project management disciplines and the correct involvement of people.

Just as failure in this area of project management is well documented, there are some well-proven techniques for improving and nurturing the skills of project management.

First, we need to address the competencies and capabilities of people that deliver change projects as opposed to normal operations, because they differ. We need training to help build those competencies. Most companies have found that you also need a means of coaching staff as well as training to really build the skills.

A company needs standard approaches for project management. Standards are consistent ways of doing things, repeatedly to the same level of quality; that is the way in which we reduce risk. The other way to reduce risks on projects is to try to reuse things from one project to another. We cannot reuse the whole project because each project is unique but we can reuse parts of it. We can reuse experience and knowledge, so long as projects follow consistent standards, hence many companies have developed a project management library which includes deliverables from a number of projects that can be used again on other projects in the future.

It is not enough just to help each project manager to improve. We need to help the company improve which means that your corporate processes, particularly business planning, project approval and funding, have to provide an environment for project success. Sponsors for projects also need guidance in how they should fulfil their role of providing support to the project team.

One point worth emphasizing is that where companies have made improvements in just one of these areas (for example, they have made training available or prepared some methods) they have found that this does not lead to a significant improvement in performance. We need this more comprehensive approach with its range of improvements, each of which reinforces the others.

MANAGING CHANGE

If we move on to failings where the solution is delivered, but not accepted and properly implemented into use by the business users, we are considering the techniques of change management.

Typical failures include a lack of planning for the changes that people must make, an inability to articulate a clear vision of the change so that people understand where the change process is taking them, or poor communications.

Very often we do not have enough involvement from the affected staff and consequently they do not feel enough commitment to the solution. People also need short-term successes to motivate them through change, so the lack of these (the 'big bang' change that takes a long time to deliver) is another key failure area.

These problems lead to the fear of failure, to resistance from staff who were not involved in the change process and who are not committed to the change. They lead to inertia where people are more comfortable with doing what they want to do today than changing for the future, because changing is risky.

The improvements that come from the techniques of change management are focused primarily on involving staff properly and on communicating very clearly what you are doing – so you overcome those concerns about the risk of failure, the fear of the unknown and people's natural resistance to change.

We have to be very clear about the change required. We then need to communicate very regularly and clearly with all people involved, but not just communicate with them. We need to involve them in the process of the project, specifying the goals and requirements, and accepting the solution against those requirements. We also need to set short-term goals, as no one can contribute to a multi-year change programme without losing interest. We have to be prepared to adjust our plans if the reactions of our staff differ from what we expected.

We must not focus solely on the effects of changing processes or IT systems, but must also consider the role of rewards systems, organizational structures and how we control our operation, because these help to shape people's behaviour.

We must also accept that direction from senior management is a critical requirement for the success of a change project. Guidance or instruction from senior management is important to remove some barriers to change and to ensure that the project receives the investment funds and resources required for success. Hence, in managing change, it is critical to have clear sponsorship and a governance process that ensures that this sponsorship is exhibited when needed and that any other senior stakeholders are supportive of the project (or at least have their concerns properly managed).

DELIVERING BUSINESS BENEFITS

The third area of failure is that our people accept the solution and they are using their new processes, procedures or IT solution, but we are still not getting the benefits that we desired when we set off on this project.

This could simply be because the business case was wrong from the start: the business case was either mistaken or it was a pet project which some senior manager was undertaking because they wanted to do it for personal reasons rather than for a clear business case. This does happen but I would suggest not too often.

It could be that the desired benefits are not properly understood or they cannot be measured. This is more frequent these days. As our businesses become more complex and change at a faster pace, it becomes more difficult to baseline the level at which the existing operation is performing. It is then harder to construct a base from which we can measure the benefit of the changes we make. A typical example is that projects claim in their original business case that they are going to improve the level of customer satisfaction, but there is often no way of accurately measuring customer satisfaction.

Therefore there is no way of baselining our performance and comparing it later to see if the project actually succeeded and contributed to improved performance.

Increasingly, the biggest cause of the failure to produce benefits is not that the benefits case was wrong at the start of the project; it is that the business environment outside of the project has changed during the life cycle of the project. This could either be that the company strategy has changed or the marketplace outside of the company has changed. Because the project has its own momentum, we cannot effectively adjust the project and the result is that we carry on with a project that is no longer the best use of our funds and resources.

In other words, when we see that the project is failing to deliver its benefits the main problem is not necessarily the failure of the project but more likely that the company has moved on from where it was when the project started. The target has moved! Solving this problem so that we are able to react to changes in the environment requires the techniques of benefits management.

Benefits management seeks to clearly articulate the benefits of the project investment. How do the deliverables from the project (perhaps a new process or technology solution) lead to an enhanced business capability (perhaps the ability to serve customers better or differentiate from competitors) and how does this capability in turn lead to a positive business outcome (perhaps improved revenue or reduced customer attrition)? Benefits management seeks to make these connections clear and compelling, rather than matters of intuition and hope.

If we implement a more structured approach to managing the benefits of each project, then we can also prioritize more effectively between competing investments (Chapter 4 looks at how benefits management underpins the concept of change programmes, which are management frameworks for the better management of business benefits, while Chapter 5 shows how the prioritization of project investments can be taken across the organization).

CONCLUSIONS

So we have reasons for failure of change projects in three stages:

- solutions not being properly delivered, where the focus is on project management failings, in terms of skills and disciplines;

- solutions not being readily accepted by our staff into operation where the problems relate to change management resulting from poor communications and involvement of staff;

- problems relating to the delivery of benefits, increasingly due to the fact that the business world outside of the projects has changed and we were unable to reflect those changes in the projects.

In these three areas, where can we put our effort to make the most difference in our project delivery performance? With about 40 per cent failure rates at each stage, it is no surprise that the answer is that we need to put our efforts in all three areas.

It would be no good, for example, to improve project management skills where the benefits case for a project is not clear. We could just be doing a better job of delivering the wrong solution.

Improving change management is not going to be the answer if our solution delivery and our project management are poor because we will have nothing to accept into operation. Better management of business benefits on its own is not the answer. If the solution delivery and change management are poor we will have nothing to produce the benefits.

We need to improve in all three areas to allow business change projects to succeed more often. From the earlier description of problems in project delivery and their remedies we are looking to create an organization with the following characteristics.

Key Characteristics of Companies that Excel in Project Delivery

- discipline, process and skills for planning projects

- strong linkage to business strategy, with realistic objectives and benefits

- careful management of key project resources

- clear communications to stakeholders

- good risk management, with lessons learnt

- issues and decisions made objectively and with collective responsibility

- management commitment and sponsorship

- empowered project managers

- emphasis on quality assurance.

While the earlier analysis of project failures cannot be considered mathematically precise, it gives us a basis from which we can design a set of measures that can improve a company's performance – a project management framework. The analysis also demonstrates that this framework must address solution delivery, change and benefits and this is a significant change of emphasis from frameworks in projectized organizations which focus most heavily on solution delivery.

2 A FRAMEWORK FOR IMPROVING PROJECT DELIVERY

The proposed framework is shown in Figure 3.3. The challenges with project delivery will vary by organization, so the emphasis on each part of the framework will also vary, but it is critical that all parts of the framework are addressed to some degree. Investing in only some parts of the framework in isolation is unlikely to improve performance in a sustainable manner.

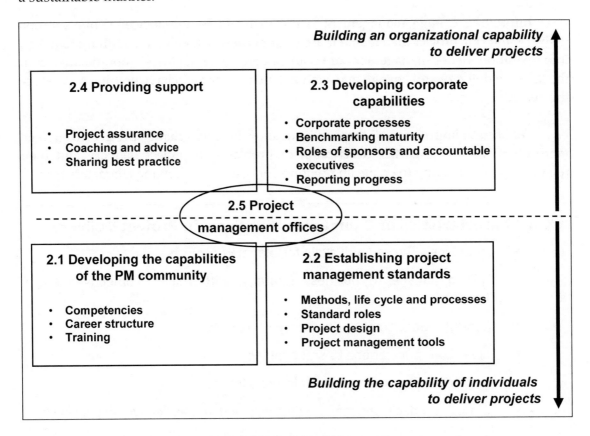

Figure 3.3   Project management framework

2.1   DEVELOPING THE CAPABILITIES OF THE PROJECT MANAGEMENT COMMUNITY

Competencies and career structure

Projects are about change. In any BAU organization, we undertake many projects as we continually seek to change the organization and gain competitive advantage by:

- launching new products to new markets;
- improving the ways we do business:
    - to be more responsive to customer needs and market trends;
    - to be more coordinated in our contact with customers;
    - to operate at lower cost;

The Role of the Project Manager

The project manager delivers the project on behalf of the business represented by an accountable executive who understands the business objectives of the project and must have a clear vision of how to achieve and measure those objectives. While the accountable executive will own the business case, the project manager has a joint responsibility to monitor it and alert others to potential changes.

The project manager agrees on the scope, budget and timescale of the project with the accountable executive and is responsible for the project achieving these. He or she must ensure the implementation remains within the agreed scope by exerting disciplined change control and must guard against risk from scope changes.

A key part of the project manager's role is to face outwards from the project, identifying and surfacing political conflicts and issues and ensuring that they are resolved by the accountable executive and others and do not impede the project. The project manager reports regularly on project status and issues to all stakeholders.

The project manager is responsible for planning the project and creating the project management plan. He or she identifies and locates the resources required for determining and delivering the solution and works with appropriate stakeholders to get commitment to obtaining the resources. The project manager monitors and reports the project's progress against the plan and budget.

Leadership and motivation of the team, often in challenging situations, is an essential part of the role. The project manager must form the team, allocate work and provide direction to the team. He or she should also support their career development and manage their release from the project. The project manager develops and maintains a communications plan covering team members and stakeholders.

The project manager contributes to the assessment of external suppliers to the project. They will expect to approve the selection, be involved in the contractual discussions with the selected suppliers and will be primarily responsible for the direct management of the suppliers throughout the life of the project.

The project manager considers known risks and dependencies (arising either from the project's scope or from the wider business environment) in the project plan and continually monitors risk during the project, setting contingency plans where required.

The project manager is responsible for ensuring that quality control and assurance are performed as required so as to achieve the deliverables. These deliverables will include regulatory and legal requirements.

The project manager develops plans for the smooth handover of the project to operational staff. They will support the accountable executive in establishing plans for the realization of benefits and will close down the project, ensuring that lessons learnt are captured for use on future projects.

- taking advantage of new channels to market;

- acquiring or disposing of business interests;

- responding to regulatory requirements;

- re-engineering processes or organizational structures.

These business projects nearly always change the way in which people work, the ways in which the organization operates and the manner in which we do business. Most projects include people from a number of different functions or disciplines and a number of locations. Most projects also include an element of technology change. All projects have some risk.

So, the project manager has to integrate the efforts of people from different disciplines in order to achieve a change that supports business strategy. Consequently, it is not surprising that many of the core competencies of a project manager are the same as for those of a general manager.

However, projects are not the same as operational activities. Each project is unique, with a start and end date and very specific objectives. Each project has a life cycle that requires different controls and processes than are appropriate for an operational activity. The project team has to be formed, maintained and disbanded with a speed far greater than for an operational activity.

Projects change the status quo in significant ways, whereas operational groups generally seek to create change in small increments.

These special features of the project environment mean that people assigned as project managers must have a discrete set of competencies, which are described in Table 3.1.

The table can be used as the basis for assessing project managers (and there are many models available, so I do not profess mine to be the best, merely one that I have found useful and practical).

The competencies, with relevant experience, can also be used to articulate a job family for project managers, recognizing the increased level of competency required as projects become larger or more complex.

Such a family can only be a guide because:

- Some individuals might qualify because of greater experience in one area and less in another.

- Different types of project require a different emphasis on skills, personal attributes and experience (for example, some projects will require a high level of content knowledge on the part of the project manager while others will not).

Table 3.1   Project management competencies

Developing the business case for projects	Defining business cases Shaping a project, its objectives and its strategies for success Securing finance Participating in benefits tracking
Specifying and managing requirements for project deliverables	Producing and gaining stakeholder agreement to specifications Controlling scope changes to ensure that project objectives are not jeopardized Ensuring that regulatory requirements are met
Developing project management plans and estimating resources	Developing a work breakdown structure Establishing the project life cycle, developing project plans and designing the project structure Estimating resources and recommending the means of procuring resources Creating plans for change management activities
Managing project governance and stakeholders	Stakeholder analysis, operation of governance/steering processes Communication and reporting Issue management Setting and managing expectations Observing corporate policies and procedures
Securing resources	Securing personnel to implement the project Establishing the project's working environment (tools, facilities)
Managing procurement	Establishing a procurement strategy Reviewing and selecting suppliers, approving contractual arrangements Managing suppliers through to acceptance and transition to maintenance or support services
Managing risk on projects	Identifying and tracking potential risks and evaluating means to mitigate them Managing funds allocated for risks and contingency
Managing teams and individuals to achieve objectives	Allocating work and agreeing objectives Monitoring and evaluating the work and providing feedback on performance Providing leadership and direction Managing conflict Maintaining morale Managing the movement of staff into and out of the project
Managing the implementation stage	Establishing management procedures for solution delivery and change management Monitoring and controlling the schedule, expenditure, risks and issues Taking corrective action as required Ensuring that quality objectives are achieved and that legal and regulatory requirements are satisfied Managing the acceptance process and an ordered handover to operational functions
Evaluating project performance	Assessing project performance against the business case and objectives Providing information to improve the estimation of future projects Distributing learning points and examples of good practice to the project team and to the project management community

- The size of project will vary by organization and industry sector.

- Finally, of course, the needs of each organization and its human resources policies for grading staff will vary.

The Roles in a Project Management Job Family

The following four roles will typically exist within the project management job family:

Project manager
Manages projects, or sub-projects, that are primarily single discipline (for example, a software application, technology infrastructure or the change management element of a larger project). Sponsorship is uncomplicated or managed by others. Project size could be up to £1 million and could involve external suppliers on simple contract terms. Internal teams could comprise up to ten people. Project risk category is low (see later in this chapter and Appendix 4 for the definition of these risk categories).

Could also take the role of project office manager on a larger project.

Senior project manager
Manages projects that are multi-discipline (for example, the change of a transaction process including new technology and some limited change activities). Projects could cover several countries but are unlikely to cover more than one functional business. Project sponsorship is relatively concentrated. Project size could be up to £3 million and the project is likely to involve external suppliers, still on relatively simple contract terms. Internal teams could comprise up to 20 people. Project risk category is low or medium.

Could manage a single discipline sub-project on a larger project or alternatively a number of small assignments. Could also take the role of project office manager on a larger project or programme.

Project director
Manages projects that are multi-discipline. The projects cover either several country operations or more than one functional business, but are unlikely to cover both. Projects are likely to be of strategic importance to one or two functional business or several country operations. The project will have a number of stakeholders and the sponsor will probably be at one level below the board. Projects will include some business change element. Project size could be up to £20 million and could involve multiple suppliers, some of whom are retained on bespoke contractual terms. Internal teams could comprise up to 50 people. Project risk category is medium or high.

Could also manage a large project that is a part of a business change programme or alternatively a portfolio of related smaller projects.

Programme manager/director
Manages a major programme of change that is of strategic importance to the organization. The programme will comprise a number of significant projects. The accountable executive is probably at one level below the board, the sponsor is at board level and the programme will have multiple stakeholders and will include significant business change. It is likely to include an element of ongoing operations. Programme size will be greater than £15 million and will involve

multiple suppliers and/or consortia, some of which are retained on complex contractual terms. The programme manager will have a significant role in the strategic relationship with the suppliers. Internal teams could be larger than 50 people. Risk category is high.

Other positions

The position of project office manager can be created either on a project (where the role is to provide the project manager with support for planning, project control and administration) or within a business function (where the role is to provide coordination of priorities, resources and dependencies across a portfolio of projects and to consolidate management reporting).

It is clear that appropriate experience and competencies are important to be able to deliver complex projects successfully, but there are a number of personal attributes that are equally important. The following panel describes these in a concise manner.

Key Attributes for Project Managers

The project manager faces two central challenges:

1. Deciding what to do, despite uncertainty, risk and an enormous amount of potentially relevant information; and

2. Getting things done, through a diverse set of internal people and external suppliers, despite having limited direct control over them.

The first challenge requires a series of personal skills and attributes while the second requires a series of interpersonal skills and attributes.

Deciding what to do:

- Shows common sense – not so common as might be expected when the pressure is on.

- Is organized – shows administrative ability, can control high volumes of concurrent, inter-related tasks.

- Is future focused – only the future can be controlled.

- Shows judgment – is objective and takes a pragmatic approach to decision making when faced with much data and several possible courses of action.

- Does not lose sight of the big picture – keeps in mind key objectives and issues and remains focused on his or her customers' needs.

- Understands key project management techniques, tools and methodologies.

- Has a working knowledge of finance, accounting, contract law and commercial practices; is commercially aware.

- Has an awareness of the business functions and technologies involved on the project.

Getting others to do it:

- Leads the team – is an integrator, bringing in a variety of people from different areas into a cohesive multi-disciplined team.

- Exerts power by gaining the respect of team members, not by reliance on hierarchical power.

- Is decisive when action is needed or decisions have to be forced.

- Shows drive, stamina and stability under pressure.

- Matches management style to situation – uses appropriate selling, negotiation and conflict-handling skills.

- Communicates effectively – to a wide range of individuals, displays empathy and a range of communication styles.

- Is sensitive to culture and politics – is adaptable, creates common objectives, searches for the win-win.

- Generates a team atmosphere that is a balance between task and fun.

(This description of a project manager's challenges could apply in any industry, but it is intended to reflect the uncertainty and limited control applying within change projects in BAU organizations. Delivering projects in such organizations can be an uncomfortable role, an exposed position subject to political interests and with inevitable conflicts where the process of project delivery overlaps with the responsibilities of BAU line managers.)

Training

There is a wide range of options available for training in project management skills – many providers with well-proven curricula. The needs for each organization will differ and cultural differences will also affect the style of training that will work best, so this book will not attempt to be specific about the training curriculum. In addition, and later in this chapter, some propositions will be made that should significantly change how training is delivered in BAU organizations.

Nevertheless, to complete the discussion of the capabilities of the individuals in the project management community, we should make some observations about project management training.

The spine of any curriculum for project management includes a number of courses or other educational experiences that cover the key principles of projects and project management, then outline the processes and approaches that are used to take a project through its life cycle. The basic course will usually be focused on the more technical aspects of planning and controlling a project (deciding what to do, as we termed it earlier) with more advanced courses bringing in the softer side of project management. We called this 'getting others to do it', with themes of team building and leadership. At the highest end of this core curriculum, the focus will be on the challenges of leading complex change initiatives that might include multiple projects and be visible at board level.

Typical training curricula will then have various more specialized training to support this core curriculum:

- more detailed techniques of planning and control

- using software tools for project control

- techniques for smaller projects

- managing information systems projects

- managing change

- managing the business case

- leadership in projects

- project finance

- contract management.

There is a tendency for off-the-shelf training curricula to make some assumptions. It is often assumed that the attendee at the course is a regular participant in projects and will, over time, be attending a number of events within the curriculum as a part of career development in a project management career path. The attendee is assumed to have the opportunity to practise the acquired skills on a frequent basis. Non-technical aspects of project management, such as managing change and stakeholders, receive limited attention until the more advanced levels of education are achieved.

When designing a curriculum for a BAU organization, it is critical that the training needs analysis questions these assumptions. First of all there will be several target audiences that need varying levels of knowledge about project management and their unique needs must be addressed:

- Will the sponsors of projects need specific education and/or coaching that reflects their role (and the limited time that they can allocate)?

- While their curricula might be based on common foundations, might business project managers and technology project managers require different attention?

- Do managers in general need some form of education (project management for non-project managers, as I have seen it called)?

- Are there other communities that need education (perhaps the annual graduate intake – the senior managers of tomorrow)?

The organization should also consider carefully the reason for problems in the delivery of its projects; in particular the balance between the individual and organizational capabilities as described in the project management framework. This will ensure that the training investment is made where it can deliver the best return.

Subject, of course, to the specific needs of the organization, I propose that the following subjects typically need a very clear focus in the curriculum when the target is a BAU organization:

- designing project organizations (see later in this chapter)

- project governance

- managing suppliers

- managing change

- realizing business benefits

- finance for project managers.

Each of these is a skill that is either crucial to the overall success of the project or is a skill where BAU organizations are weak when compared with projectized organizations.

A key decision is whether the more basic courses should be based around the organization's own project management standards or industry standards. If the organization has invested in developing a methodology then it seems wasteful to miss out on the opportunity of training aspiring project managers in the specific methods.

Another key decision is whether the organization wishes to invest in a rolling programme of building project management skills or will focus its training on project teams who are about to embark on a live business project. The latter provides just-in-time training with immediate application. The training is often conducted as a form of project definition workshop that helps the project team develop the plans and management approaches for their own project. If there is also some form of aftercare coaching this approach can be very effective in improving project performance.

This approach requires a commitment of time and money at project initiation that can be hard to justify to project sponsors on a case-by-case basis, so it is best justified as a generic approach that is shown to deliver a better return on investment than a rolling programme (when one can never be sure that the right people are being trained or that they have the opportunity to apply the skills soon after).

2.2   ESTABLISHING PROJECT MANAGEMENT STANDARDS

Methods, life cycle and processes

It is not the purpose of this book to develop or describe a project management methodology in detail; many others have done justice to the subject and professional bodies of knowledge carry on the development work. My main concern is practical implementation of a methodology that project staff will recognize as delivering added value. In a BAU organization, this inevitably means that the methodology must be less specialist and complex than is the case in projectized organizations. This simpler approach should not be read as the adoption of a less robust project management process, but must recognize that BAU organizations will be less tolerant of complex methods than will projectized organizations. BAU organizations also have less repeatability in their projects than do projectized organizations.

A further challenge is to develop a methodology that can be used for a wide range of projects – everything from integrating an acquired company to moving office premises to re-engineering business processes to implementing new technology infrastructure.

Distilled down to its essentials, any project management methodology has to comprise:

- a life cycle of project phases;

- processes that are used to control the project as it moves through the life cycle;

- a means of assessing risk, so that the control processes can be made less or more rigorous to suit the level of risk;

- standard descriptions of the key roles required for the delivery of a project.

Many forms of life cycle exist, each in some way reflecting the culture of the host organization. Figure 3.4 depicts some variants. For business change projects and this book I will use the version listed last in Figure 3.4:

- *Business planning* – a concept for a project is born, either as a necessary enabler of business growth or as a response to a business problem.

- *Feasibility* – the project is assessed to see that the business need can be satisfied at an acceptable cost and risk. Management approval leads to the next phase of activity.

- *Detailed planning* – the business case and the project to deliver the solution are shaped in more detail. Again, management approval sanctions the increased level of expenditure that will be needed in the next phase.

- *Implementation* – the solution is delivered.

- *Transition and project closure* – the results of the project are handed over to BAU operations and responsibility.

- *Business operations* – the benefits of the investment in the project are received.

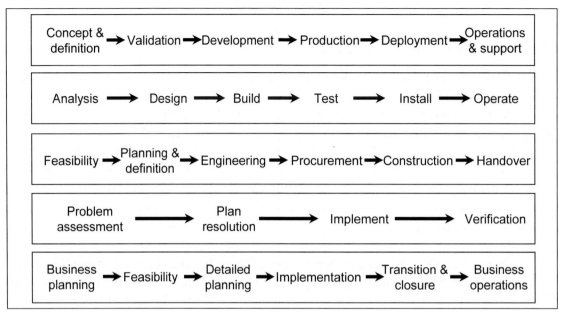

Figure 3.4   Project life cycle

My recommended set of control processes is described in Figure 3.5. One would see a similar set of processes in any methodology, so there is no rocket science here, but there are some differences when compared with formal methodologies adopted in projectized organizations or texts that address projectized organizations. The three processes shown at the top of Figure 3.5 are governance, business acceptance of change and benefits management, all key to the successful management of business change. I support these processes with attention to the processes of project initiation, planning and ongoing control.

Finally, these are supported by the management of cost, quality, people and procured services – all processes designed to make the best use of assets at the project's disposal.

Compared with projectized organizations, there is a shift in this depiction of the processes, in that it regards the business rationale for the project and the management of change as pre-eminent, attracting more focus than the processes that address solution delivery. Business acceptance is not a stage in the life cycle (as implied in solution-oriented methodologies) but a process running throughout the life cycle.

For each of these control processes, we can describe the key actions and outputs that are required for good project management and I have included these in Appendix 1. They are called minimum control standards as they provide the essential framework for the control of the project. Any other measures required for a specific project will be added to this list of minimum standards.

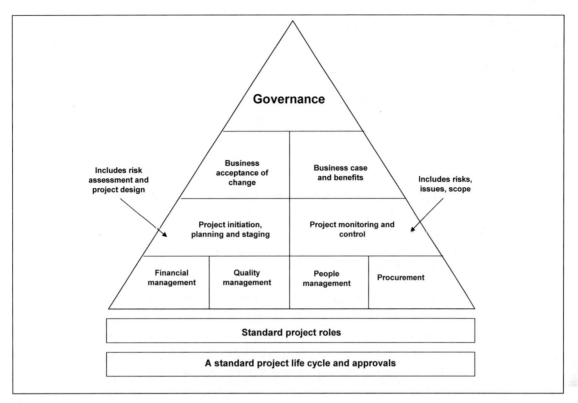

Figure 3.5   Control processes

This level of methodology is simple to explain and relevant to a wide range of projects. Many of the processes are well-established in any project methodology and require no amplification here. I have made an exception for the key processes of managing stakeholders in support of business change and of managing business benefits, and Appendices 2 and 3 provide some notes on techniques.

The risk assessment of a project, undertaken in the feasibility and detailed planning stages, is described in Appendix 4. This assesses projects as low, medium or high risk based upon a number of measures that are appropriate for the particular BAU organization.

As a project becomes more complex or risky, then we should expect that the management approach also becomes more sophisticated. So, for example, every project needs a communications plan but its content and formality will vary widely depending upon project size and complexity. Similarly, the processes to control the project must become more robust as project risk increases, in particular the processes for project approval, governance and assurance. Every project needs an appropriate governance body, but the role of such bodies and the seniority of their participants will also vary widely by project. Appendix 4 also shows how this increased rigour for riskier projects is applied, but still within the same methodology.

We do not clutter up the methodology by trying to prescribe in fine detail what must be in the communications plan, to use the same example again, and we accept that such plans will vary hugely between various projects. If we try to explain how communications plans look for projects of differing complexity this will complicate the methodology (methodologies in projectized organizations often show how each process or document looks in a variety of projects, which is neat and intellectually robust, but very complicated).

The best way to show how the rigour and detail of a project process or document changes with project risk and complexity is simply to include various model examples within the project library (see later).

Finally, I should note that, expressed in this way as a master methodology and based upon standard processes, it is still possible where required to adopt a more specific and prescribed methodology for components of the project (software development life cycles being a common example).

Standard roles on projects

In support of a standard life cycle and set of control processes, the project management approach must also include a standard set of key roles. Without this, we would have to think through the roles on a project each time from first principles and this would hugely increase the risk of confusion and project failure. The roles, like the processes, are a form of stability that anchors the project as it proceeds through its risky life cycle.

In hard projects, there are typically two key roles – that of the sponsor, who creates the need for the project and desires its deliverables, together with the project manager who delivers the project solution to the sponsor's requirements. In softer projects the goal of the project is oriented to a stream of future benefits (owned by a relevant line manager who must be held clearly accountable for the return on the project investment). Furthermore, the political nature of change projects in relatively hierarchical organizations demands a sponsor who is at a relatively senior place in the organization. These twin demands lead us to create a third role – that of the accountable executive who is responsible for the business case of the project, its business requirements and the ownership of the project's deliverables and benefits after the project solution has been delivered. If we were working in the construction industry we might call this person the 'operator'. The sponsor's role becomes more strategic – approving the desired business benefits and setting the project's success criteria, validating that the project is aligned to strategic goals (and monitoring that it remains so as the business environment changes) and gaining corporate buy-in to the project and its associated investment costs.

The project manager remains as the single point of responsibility for delivering the project's solution, defining the project scope, planning and leading the project team.

This triumvirate of key roles is consistent with current thinking on large-scale programmes of change, where the need for an owner of benefits, discrete from the overall sponsor, is being recognized. In my opinion, the same needs apply for a single project so as to have a balanced set of responsibilities, skills and interests and the triumvirate of roles provides this (see Figure 3.6).

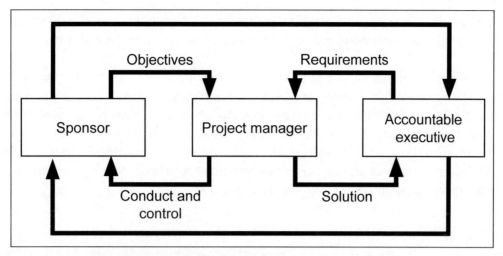

Figure 3.6   Three key project roles

Inevitably, a form of hierarchy operates between sponsor, accountable executive and project manager, but the description of the three roles as complementary, each delivering something to the others, is intended to make the relationships more task-focused and hence improve the objectivity of decision making on the project.

An accountable executive in a BAU organization faces some key conflicts:

- managing ongoing BAU activity in parallel to playing his or her leadership role on the project;

- balancing budgets between BAU and the project (often the organization's financial controls do not segregate these very well, unlike in projectized organizations);

- personal conflict of interest – wanting the project to deliver well but not wanting to increase the BAU profit targets by the budget amount – human nature!

The sponsor has a key role in helping the accountable executive manage these conflicts.

The roles of the sponsor and accountable executive span the entire life cycle of the project, from business planning through to business operations. While the project manager might be retained for a shorter period, it is critical that they are appointed early enough to share in the personal accountability for successful delivery and to use project management disciplines to shape the project correctly. Far too many projects in BAU organizations have failed because the project manager was appointed late and did not feel ownership for the business case, or arrived when a flawed solution and project design were already in place. Assign the project manager very early.

No matter how emotionally committed are the sponsor and accountable executive to the project, they are both people with other (BAU) responsibilities and demands on their time. It falls to the project manager to ensure, or prompt others to ensure, that stakeholders, change and benefits are managed; hence the focus earlier upon the organizational, political and personal competencies as well as technical skills.

A common failing is that sponsors are involved early, but inadequately (often restricted to signing off the investment) and so do not contribute their strategic perspective to the project in its critical early stages. Alternatively, the sponsor disengages from the project once the investment is approved. In both cases the end result is that they spend a lot more time on the project later on, as part of efforts to rescue a project that is failing to deliver! Project managers and accountable executives must use steering committees and any other means at their disposal to keep sponsors engaged.

Project design

To those of us who have worked in projectized organizations, this skill is a natural part of how projects are managed. We analyze the project's deliverables through a work breakdown structure (WBS) and consider the organizational implications (an organizational breakdown structure, OBS). Then we consider how the project structure will have to recognize political considerations: do we have the right means of engaging stakeholders, do we have the right participants on governance bodies and in the project team?

A large project was underway to move all of a bank's staff into a single new office facility. Tasks related to the tangible deliverables of the project were well underway (office fit-out, technology infrastructure, regulatory and legal conditions) but a project review, based upon a WBS analysis, demonstrated that there was a further deliverable that was not being explicitly addressed – satisfied staff, without which the proposed efficiency savings of the new office would not be realized.

In order to achieve this product from the project, a number of additional deliverables were required. Some related purely to staff perceptions (communications, transport arrangements) but others had an impact upon the wider scope of the project. A redesign of the staff dining area was agreed to compensate for negative perceptions of the office location and this required a significant redesign of the building layout.

The analysis also changed the way in which staff functions were engaged on the project, and the steering forum that oversaw the project was broadened to include a wider selection of staff.

WBS is a powerful tool in designing change projects, not well enough applied by project teams in BAU organizations.

If I were to highlight one fundamental difference between the practised project manager and the novice, it would be this ability to consider the project and the project process and to construct the structure in a way that balances multiple demands. This is a complex organizational design task, part logical and part political, and in business change projects the project manager must proceed with care, since the design that best suits the project in a technical sense might not suit all stakeholders.

In BAU organizations, this skill of project design is not well appreciated. Furthermore, it is rarely acknowledged that the structure will have to evolve as we move through the project life cycle. On most projects, the structure and key resources are set during the early feasibility stages, but the team in place is likely to be inappropriate for the later stages, when implementation and broad stakeholder engagement will be the focus of activity.

A detailed appraisal of different project structures is outside the scope of this book, but we can outline some typical considerations that will help the project manager to design an appropriate structure.

Task force, matrix or functional

The first consideration is the traditional one of considering project structures by assessing how they relate to BAU functions. Classical project teams are formed on a task force basis, where they are segregated from BAU and dedicated to one project. The project manager acts as both task manager and line manager for the staff for the time that they are allocated to the project. The other extreme is a functional model, where the projects are conducted by a much looser association of staff who are still owned and managed within their home, functional departments. In between these options is the matrix model, where staff might share their time across BAU and project activities or across multiple projects. In the matrix, the project manager instructs staff on what to do, by when and within what budget, whereas the line, functional manager instructs staff on how long they should be allocated to the project and to what technical standards they should conduct their work.

Task force approaches offer the highest level of organizational focus on the goals of a project and are most appropriate when risks are high or projects are complex and of long duration. In a projectized organization, where the projects are the sum total of the business, resources are allocated from one task force to another as needed, but in a BAU organization the resources will have to be drawn from BAU tasks, which will cause disruption. A functional model reduces this problem (or does it perhaps just disperse the problem across the organization?) but is unlikely to be able to provide the same level of concerted focus on a project as a task force approach.

The matrix model tries to achieve a better balance between the project and the functional, BAU organization. It relies on many agreements being made (at the intersections of the matrix) between line managers and project managers about how work is done and by whom. This brings complexity and requires a task-focused culture, something that is not necessarily in place in financial services companies that can be quite hierarchical in nature. It is rare to find a fully-developed matrix structure in a BAU organization, except in discrete areas such as technology that deliver projects on a regular basis.

A key factor to consider is the environment in which the project is operating; if we do not want to dilute the ownership or sponsorship that a BAU function has for a project, or want to avoid transition issues as the project moves into BAU operations, or we depend critically upon the availability of resources who have ongoing BAU responsibilities, then we are likely to select a functional model over the task force or matrix approach.

Some complex projects can use a combination of models.

In 2004/5, large banks are conducting projects and programmes to become compliant with a new set of regulations called Basel II. These regulations require banks to improve their processes and analytical techniques to satisfy banking regulators that their business risk is well managed (which in turn helps to safeguard the stability of the banking sector as a whole). Managing risk is the core capability of a bank, so one could imagine that some of these enhancements to risk management techniques are just the latest in a series of continual improvements and are best conducted by the functional owners of risk management in the bank. The programme will want to oversee that progress is being made as planned, but the tasks are conducted by a functional team.

However, Basel II also requires a significant upgrade in most banks' data storage infrastructure; data warehousing projects are complex and lengthy and the task force model is likely to be most appropriate to assure the dedication of various technical staff over a lengthy period.

In an international bank, many projects within a Basel II programme will take place within an individual business unit, but there is also a need for a consistent approach across the organization as regulators will expect this consistency and the organization anyway needs a common way of working. Examples would be risk management policies and standards for data quality. These projects will necessarily have a degree of matrix management where local project owners are subject to some standardization of approach from central project managers or functional managers.

Other considerations
There are other considerations in the design of a change project, in addition to the decisions between task force, matrix and functional structures.

- Is the project global or local in nature? Do we want to start the project as an explicitly global exercise (high profile, but early progress will be slowed by multiple stakeholders and this will require a larger project team to manage communications) or start it as a local exercise that might grow in scope as the pilot implementations bear fruit (clear sponsorship early on but a danger that the solution is not optimal or capable of global deployment; hence the team will need a strong focus on solution design and scope change)?

- If a project is global, or international, or deployed in numerous business units, how much control does the central function and project team desire for confidence that the project will be successful? Can the project be devolved to business units, in line with an agreed design with relatively low risk (an example being the roll-out of a new brand identity across the company)? If not, can a slightly more centralized model be used, where business units undertake the implementation in line with some form of template plan, to provide greater control of the outcome. Finally, does the central team want to impose even stronger control, with feedback and reporting from business units that they have implemented as intended (maybe even with some assurance from the centre)? The latter is likely on projects that deliver regulatory compliance. This balance of control is a critical decision point on most complex, multi-business projects.

- Can the project be delivered as a series of stages, or must it be tackled as one delivery? If the project can be handled as stages (with the obvious benefits of reducing risk) should the stages be based upon serial implementations in different countries or business units, or the roll-out of functionality in a staged manner? Should some form of pilot implementation be used? Can business benefits be generated early by the deployment of a temporary solution? See Appendix 5 for some notes on the use of stages in change projects.

- How clear are the goals of the project? Will they evolve over time? Will different skills and organizational contacts be required as the project evolves?

- What will be the appropriate culture on the project? In the brand identity project mentioned above, it became clear to the central project team that so much enthusiasm was being generated in country business units that a general attempt at controlling detailed tasks from the centre would fail. A risk-based approach was taken, whereby most country business units were left to their own devices (the risk of problems that could not be easily remedied being considered low) and only larger business units were subject to central control. In contrast, regulatory projects demand very low failure rates and, being less exciting and not revenue-generating, are more prone to staff being withdrawn or to short cuts, so a more tightly controlled approach is appropriate.

- Is the project centred around technology-based change or process-based change? Where do we get the best return on our management time?

- Will parts of the project that are sourced externally be subject to traditional procurement (client/supplier) or are more innovative approaches possible (approaches that might require a closer partnership and shared objectives, either of which will require careful consideration of the skills and behaviours of the client team).

All of these considerations affect the final design of the project – a design that reflects the culture of the organization and the project, the risks and inevitably the skills and behaviours of the people associated with the project.

Project management tools

It is outside the scope of this book to describe project management tools in detail. In any case the market moves fast enough that specific comments date quickly. However, there are some observations that are important in applying project management tools in BAU organizations.

These observations flow from both the nature of change projects and the culture of BAU organizations. On a business change project, we certainly have the challenges of managing deliverables, costs, resources, dependencies, risks and project benefits and here we could ideally rely upon traditional project management tools that are based upon critical path analysis and resource allocation.

However, many of the key challenges on the project are not logistical but based upon the engagement of a disparate community of stakeholders and the timely allocation of specialized experts or business users to the project. Dependencies that are serious enough to worry the project manager are relatively obvious on all but the most complex of exercises.

These differences reduce the added value of the traditional tools.

Their value is also diluted by the disparate nature of the community of stakeholders, many of whom do not fit the traditional picture of a team member or project manager. These participants each have their own, unique requirements for the content and format of information – information that is relevant to their piece of the project. They want information that is filtered and prioritized according to their needs and provided at a level of detail that suits them.

Bar charts, which are so intuitive to the project manager, are just not compelling to many staff in BAU organizations – something that comes as a shock to career project managers when they realize it! This issue further limits the value of the more traditional tools that are based upon critical path methodologies.

Team members also want information that is not wrapped in the bureaucracy of heavyweight project progress reports but is made available, in isolation, for them. Think of this as a BAU in-tray. For many participants on a project, there is limited need or desire for them to have knowledge across the project. They want to see just the pieces that require them to be informed or take action, just like all the other BAU tasks that enter their in-tray. This makes project control feel less specialist or bureaucratic and this is more likely to create good engagement from participants.

As projects are typically cross-functional (and increasingly international) the tools that we use should facilitate the transfer of information. Collaboration and the efficient management of knowledge are essential if project teams are to be formed, informed and controlled in short timescales.

If we wish to achieve this speed of information transfer, we also need a solution that uses existing and varied data from various sources without the need for complex reprocessing or integration. It will include some easily accessible repository of project information (not just about costs and resources, but a library of key documentation).

Hence, when looking for a toolset to support a change project, we need to carefully assess the requirements and in particular the balance between control and collaboration. With this balance in mind, today's trend is to seek tools that complement project management capabilities with knowledge management and collaboration across a community of interested parties. They are more user-centric than traditional tools, are typically browser-based and have user-friendly presentation. They bring together the elements of project control (tasks, milestones, financial data, resources, risk and issues) but match these with facilities for knowledge sharing, collaboration and accountability. Because they are built upon the concept of a user community, they are designed to tailor the information that is presented to each member of the community.

Typical solutions, progressively more complex, include:

- simple web-based project reporting tools;

- workgroup collaboration tools, often built on database or email solutions;

- virtual team rooms, where users can set up a shared space for information, prepare and display project plans and control participation (solutions that are available on a hosted, user-priced basis);

- knowledge management tools with more sophisticated functions for distributing information (for example, actions and alerts) but typically quite basic project control capabilities;

- project management portals, typically with similar capabilities to knowledge management tools but with increased emphasis on project control and sometimes with coverage of benefits and change management processes as well as core project control processes.

2.3 DEVELOPING CORPORATE CAPABILITIES

Corporate processes

If it is to be successful, the organization's approach to project delivery must include a number of corporate processes that are supportive of projects. As outlined in Chapter 2, these processes are natural in projectized organizations but in BAU organizations they have to be modified to suit the delivery of projects.

The most obvious example is the process used to approve project funding. This process usually evolves out of a BAU process for setting annual budgets; as a result it usually fails to recognize the life cycle through which a project evolves and does not reflect the high level of uncertainty in a project's estimates when they are made in the early stages of the life cycle. There is little recognition that projects should return regularly for re-approval, that cost, time and quality are not independent parameters but subject to trade-offs, or that the level of project risk and contingency will affect the project approach and outcome. One of the first moves in improving project delivery is to start changing the corporate process for funding projects (and to do this one step at a time so that the organization does not reject a wholesale change).

The corporate process for tracking project progress is closely related to project funding and it will typically need to be modified to reflect the same themes of uncertainty and risk management. As we covered in Chapter 2, BAU organizations can display behaviours that are inconsistent with the needs of projects and this process is a visible way to change these behaviours.

One of the key subjects to consider in the funding and tracking processes (as this leads to improved behaviour in various ways) is the use of estimating allowances and contingency (simplistically the former is to cater for known imperfections in how the project is estimated, the latter is a broader allowance for unforeseen circumstances). If the champion of project management can introduce these concepts into corporate processes (without them being perceived as padding to estimates) then they can be used to change management behaviour as they force a regular re-appraisal of project risk, timescale and cost and embed a concept of uncertainty in forecasts.

Other key, BAU corporate processes that need to be changed to include projects are:

- tracking the delivery of business benefits, which we will discuss in Chapters 4 and 5;

- the clear allocation of delegated authorities to project managers for approving contracts, invoices, internal resources and project changes. As project managers exist partly outside BAU hierarchies, they can be left out here, with a detrimental effect on their empowerment;

- human resources processes, which need to ensure that resources who are seconded on to projects are not forgotten by their home BAU department, that their performance on the project is properly assessed and rewarded and that their return to a BAU role is well managed. Where reward is a key aspect of the culture (such as bonus payments in financial services), secondments to a back room role on a project are particularly hard to arrange unless project-based bonus arrangements are put in place.

Benchmarking maturity

It is a corporate responsibility to track how the organization's capability to deliver projects is improving. The assessment of an organization's maturity and/or competency is a topic currently attracting much attention and there are a number of maturity models available through consultancies and professional institutions. It is outside the scope of this book to compare them but some form of benchmarking is a key part of any project management framework.

When seconded BAU managers lead change projects, it is particularly useful to use the maturity benchmarks as a means to promote discipline and consistency in approach.

Roles of sponsors and accountable executives

There are some aspects of project delivery in BAU organizations that will appear in more than one guise in the project management framework. The repetition is intentional, for these aspects are critical to project success. One example is the skill of designing the project structure and another is the governance and leadership of business change. We have discussed governance and leadership already as a part of the skill set of the project manager, as a key process within the project management methodology and within the three standard roles that are present on any project. Now, we should discuss the corporate efforts that can support this leadership on change projects.

While sponsors and accountable executives have the skill of business leadership and peer recognition within the organization, they will not necessarily have all the skills needed to lead a project. They should be provided with awareness of these skills. If there is the appetite, training events can be provided (perhaps to an entire management team if the senior executive supports this use of their time) but this is rarely the case and subtler methods are more successful. Checklists are appreciated, as they allow these senior executives to drill into the key issues on projects without having to digest voluminous information about the project. I am in favour of issuing small booklets (easy to have at hand) that include a combination of checklists, descriptions of the project life cycle and reminders of the roles of the sponsor and accountable executive.

Questions for a Sponsor to Self-assess Performance

1. Is the project still in line with corporate strategy?

2. Are there better uses of the investment funds?

3. Are other key stakeholders being managed?

4. What challenges are likely to the project funding?

5. Is it time to publicly recognize team or individual performance?

6. When is the next independent assurance of the project?

7. What have I done to promote the project in the last three months?

8. Does the accountable executive have a clear view of the business benefits?

9. Are the benefits built into business budgets?

10. What events could change company strategy to such an extent that the project should be re-evaluated?

Questions for an Accountable Executive to Self-assess Performance

1. What events could change the project's business case?

2. How sensitive is the business case to delays or cost over-runs?

3. Have all scope changes been properly authorized?

4. What are the project's top five risks?

5. Are all key stakeholders aware of status and issues?

6.   How much contingency is left in the schedule and budget?

7.   How are we managing change for affected staff?

8.   What is the strategy for gaining user acceptance?

9.   Do I have a clear strategy for transition of the solution into BAU?

10.   Have I decided how to track that benefits are realized?

The sponsor and accountable executive cannot govern the project without support. The role of the project steering committee (PSC) is key in securing the support of other parties and there should be a corporate process to ensure that suitable PSCs are formed. While the sponsor will have a good view of the stakeholder issues present, the project manager should supplement this by structured analysis and action plans.

Above each project, there is a need for a higher level of corporate governance and this is discussed again in Chapters 4 and 5.

Reporting progress

Senior managers need clear information about the scope, progress and risks of a project if they are to govern it well. A further corporate capability, therefore, is to present information in a way that encourages participation and consideration of the key issues. However, managers in BAU organizations rarely respond well to the types of reports that are natural in projectized organizations. Bar charts are a poor way of communicating plans, particularly if they are depicted simply as the raw output from project management tools. Benefits roadmaps might help the project team to articulate benefits, but senior managers react better to a spreadsheet. Complex descriptions or charts of team structures work less well than simple, textual terms of reference for team members.

So, if the traditional means of communicating project approach and progress do not work well in a BAU organization, what will work?

- Progress reports depicted as balanced scorecards (because line managers are used to the balanced scorecard methodology from BAU activity). A simple balanced scorecard for a project could include four quadrants as follows:

  — stewardship (notes on governance, organization, quality assurance)

  — milestones (planned, forecast, approved as completed)

  — status (achievements to date, next period plans, key risks)

  — financial (cash and profit and loss information, benefits).

- balanced scorecards can also be tailored to address the key challenges of projects. For example, when used to describe the more complex projects or a collection of projects they can focus more attention on the delivery of benefits than on deliverables; the scorecard can include graphs or tables to show the way in which benefits achieved compare with targets. If there are key performance indicators (see Appendix 2) the scorecards could include these leading indicators for visibility.

- traffic light alert systems for risks and progress (RAG, standing for red, amber, green). These can be appropriate when summarizing a number of projects for executive management or for more detailed progress reporting on a project with a large number of constituent parts (perhaps a project to roll out a new business process or product across multiple countries).

- High-level bar charts that are depicted as clear pictures (not looking like the output from a project management tool – usually just showing critical paths). An alternative treatment is to depict these without bars, simply as a series of key milestones. This provides a much simpler presentation.

- Plans presented as a gap analysis, the gap being between a current state and a future state and then showing the activities needed to fill each gap. This can be useful in conjunction with a RAG approach that would show the risk associated with closing each gap in the required time and to the required quality level. It is effective in projects for tracking compliance with new regulations, for example.

- Risk maps presented as a matrix of the probability of a risk occurring and the magnitude of its impact if it does occur.

The organization can help sponsors and accountable executives to perform well if it provides information on project progress that is clear and tailored to their preferences.

2.4 PROVIDING SUPPORT

Project assurance

Any textbook on the basic principles of project management starts by noting that each project is unique, transient and hence an uncertain and risky venture. The project team, however experienced they might be as individuals, has never delivered the same project before. An organization needs a way of independently assuring that the project is likely to achieve its objectives.

Quality assurance is typically performed as a short healthcheck review based upon project information and complemented by interviews with members of the project team. The focus is to establish that the project's plans are valid, that the members of the team have a common understanding of objectives and issues and that the risks are being mitigated. The validity of the original benefits case is checked and alternative approaches that might simplify the project are explored.

Adherence to appropriate project management disciplines will also be covered, as this will help the reviewer to assess the risk profile of the project, but it should be emphasized that the review is primarily a holistic assessment of the health of the project rather than an audit of processes.

The most popular ways of providing resource for the reviews are as follows:

1. Use a central pool of experienced project managers to conduct reviews. These experts might be part of a central centre of expertise that brings the benefits of transferring knowledge quickly between projects, but this is an expensive service and likely to come under budget pressures as an overhead in BAU organizations.

2. Where a project management office (PMO, see Section 2.5 later) is in place to monitor project progress across a business unit, it is possible to enhance the role of the PMO to include these reviews. This brings an added benefit of improving the general level of debate and engagement between the PMO and project teams, which in turn will increase the added value of the PMO. More senior, experienced resource might have to be added to the PMO to deliver this enhanced role.

3. Alternatively, a business can implement a peer review process, which uses senior, practising project managers (who are running their own projects elsewhere in the organization) to undertake the reviews. This approach helps ensure that recommendations from the reviews are practical and also creates the opportunity to share good practice between projects. Most project managers who undertake reviews find that their time is well spent because of spin-off benefits for their own project, for example by seeing how another project team is tackling similar issues.

4. Use external consultants to provide the service. While a more expensive option, this brings the benefits of introducing external best practice. It can be the most appropriate option if we regard this healthcheck skill as a scarce asset that the organization does not wish to fund as a permanent resource.

Some attention is needed to ensure that a peer review process maintains objectivity. Reviews should be coordinated through a central point such as a PMO and two project managers should not review each other's projects. Recommendations from the review must be documented and distributed to the steering committee and other stakeholders.

Coaching and advice

Just like assurance, the value of coaching for project teams is to reduce risk. Occasional advice from another project manager (a peer or from a centre of expertise) can reduce project risk and identify cheaper and faster ways to deliver the project. This coaching can be ad hoc (based upon a quality assurance review) or regular (perhaps facilitation of a project startup workshop, followed by regular reviews and more personal coaching of the project manager on key project challenges).

In the early days of improving project performance, a coaching service offers a fast way to add value to the business through practical support to live projects. The coaching service also accelerates the transfer of knowledge between projects as the coaches share knowledge between themselves.

Continuity of staff is important in such a service, but these interventions can become over-familiar very easily, ceasing to ask difficult, provocative questions. To avoid this, hold regular reviews at key milestones (when there is something concrete to discuss) and also focus coaching discussions on areas where the most benefit can be created (for example, the project design issues discussed above, which inexperienced project staff find a challenging topic – two heads are better than one on such complex design tasks). Alternatively, arrange that coaching sessions be led by external consultants to preserve independence.

Despite the great value of a central coaching service, they have a limited shelf life as they can become stale and can be seen as a corporate overhead. This usually leads one to a model based upon either peer review using internal project managers as coaches or external, consulting resources, with either type of coaching arranged through PMOs. While the model might change as the organization matures, it is essential to provide some form of coaching service if project risks are to be reduced.

Sharing best practice

As every project is unique, we cannot depend entirely on previous experience when planning and delivering projects. However, we can significantly reduce risk by ensuring that all project teams are provided with the agreed methodologies, tools, guidance and advice. We can also reduce risk by re-using the deliverables and practices that succeeded on previous projects. These could include examples of key project documents such as project management plans, communications plans, quality plans and deliverables such as specifications for IT systems. If versions of these are maintained from projects of differing size and complexity, they will help new project teams to appreciate how much detail and rigour is required for each project. Template deliverables should also be provided, based upon best practice examples, to help project teams prepare their documents quickly and to set quality standards for their work.

Most of the processes within the project management methodology are supported by techniques (how to undertake stakeholder analysis in a structured manner, as an example) and information on these should also be retained centrally.

In a projectized organization, the contents of this repository of information could also include end products from the project – pieces of software, process descriptions, and so on – but the limited repeatability of projects in BAU organizations means that these are rarely retained centrally. Projectized organizations are usually obsessive about storing and sharing post implementation reviews, but again this is less popular in BAU organizations.

These deliverables should be made available to project teams as some form of project management library, which today would usually be based on the company intranet, a project management portal or a knowledge management application.

As a location frequently visited by project teams, the library is a good place to make available the more general information about project delivery in the organization – other parts of the framework such as training events and career structures.

2.5 PROJECT MANAGEMENT OFFICES

Whenever an individual project reaches a significant size, the project manager needs some administrative support to help him or her manage the project. This support can cover a range of topics:

- planning support;
- monitoring progress, including risks and issues;
- communications project library of key documents;
- change control;
- quality assurance.

This support service, called a 'project management office' (PMO), can be considered as an extension of the project manager.

The concept of a PMO is also used in another context: as a corporate resource to assist the delivery of all the projects in an organization or division. In this broader, corporate role they are sometimes called 'programme offices'. Their roles usually fall into the following five disciplines:

- tracking the progress of projects, to assure management that projects are healthy;
- providing quality assurance (either through an expert team or the coordination of peer reviews);
- allocating resources across projects, optimizing their use and predicting future shortfalls;
- acting as a centre of expertise for project management standards, techniques and tools, a role that would usually also include responsibility for project management training and a project management library;
- improving the strategic alignment of business change projects by tracking project benefits and advising management of the best use of investment funds and other resources.

Each organization will start a PMO for its own reasons, typically linked to the key issues of the day, so while the common term of PMO is used to describe them, their roles can vary widely between organizations. Their roles are also affected by the culture of the organization, in particular the level of centralized control that is exerted by the organization's centre upon individual business units. So, organizations that are focused in one country are often quite centralized in their culture and find it useful to start their PMOs on control functions such as tracking projects, moving on later to act as centres of expertise. Some more international organizations might devolve project tracking to each subsidiary business unit, so the corporate PMO might naturally have its initial focus on setting standards and transferring knowledge.

As an organization's competency in project delivery improves, it would be natural that it might use a PMO in more of the five areas listed above. I recently conducted a benchmark review with 12 other BAU organizations, which considered their maturity by assessing processes, methodologies and organizational support for project management to arrive at an aggregate score out of 5. Scores ranged from 2.5 to 4.5. Plotting this score against the number of areas where PMOs were used results in Figure 3.7. While I could not claim this to be the most scientific or broad of surveys, the level of correlation is very good and seems to support the notion, which has been described in numerous research papers, of the corporate PMO being a centre of gravity for improving project delivery across the organization.

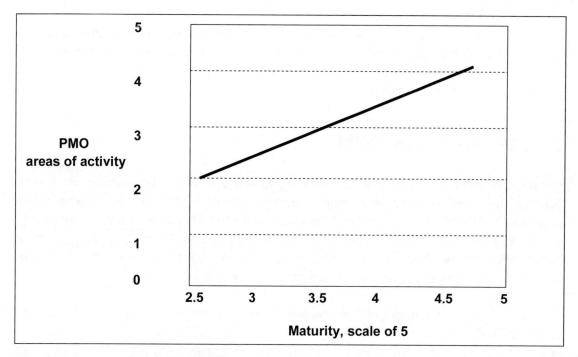

Figure 3.7   Scope of PMOs

The various roles of a PMO have implications for the skills required and this is an issue that many BAU companies are facing at the moment. PMOs that started as trackers of project progress will not have the depth of skills required to move on to coaching project managers or strategic management of project investments. If there is a well-defined project management community, then there could be opportunities for secondments into the corporate PMO as a part of knowledge transfer and career development. In any event this is a sensible resourcing strategy for a PMO to prevent it becoming remote from front-line project work.

In the early stages of a PMO's life, this approach might not be possible and interim support from consultants or fixed-term contractors should be considered.

In projectized organizations, PMOs are such a natural part of the control framework that the principle of having one is rarely questioned, but PMOs within BAU organizations can be seen as a corporate overhead, a bureaucratic and potentially threatening function serving head office. The following approaches can be useful to reduce this perception:

- secondments, as described above, to reduce costs and improve perceptions as staff move in and out of the PMO;

- transferring some PMO tasks to other, BAU functions. For example, aspects of project tracking and benefits management can be passed over to the Finance function (in which case the PMO operates in a more virtual fashion with activities embedded in other parts of the organization);

- focusing more on the higher skill tasks such as project reviews, coaching and portfolio management.

Understanding the priorities for the PMO out of a wide range of possible roles, planning how these priorities will evolve as the organization matures and then plotting a careful strategy for resourcing and funding the PMO are critical aspects of maintaining executive support. These are important considerations, since PMOs are so important as a centre of gravity for project delivery expertise.

3 MAKING IT HAPPEN

Having designed a project management framework, how do we implement this in practice? Introducing a new technique or competency such as project management is a project in itself (and a change project at that!). It needs to be conducted with sponsorship, with discipline and with careful consideration of the needs, interests and opinions of many stakeholders. You will see such an initiative described in project management journals as a project improvement programme or similar.

The first point that must be addressed is the approach to be taken on sponsorship and mandate. In any classical change initiative, we look first for clear, visible sponsorship and a mandate from senior management that 'this must happen'. However, such a clear, mandatory statement is rarely provided in practice and, even if it is, it might not be accepted universally across a broad enterprise. This is often the case when trying to improve project management, where the organization's appreciation of the competency is initially vague or perhaps accepted only by a small community within the organization.

Sometimes, a strong, public mandate can even be a problem – for example, the initiative that is from head office and to which lip service is paid without any real enthusiasm or support in other areas of the organization.

The good news is that a strong mandate is not the only means to create change. Contrary to the more traditional theories of change management, one can create change through a careful, progressive approach that guides affected people to their own conclusions and acceptance of new ways.

Let us consider two approaches to starting to introduce project management – the explicit approach and the stealthy approach.

EXPLICIT CHANGE

If we consider the framework described earlier, summarized in Figure 3.8, the explicit route to introducing project management that requires significant mandate (a CEO who has seen the light, perhaps) is based upon the imposition of project management methodologies across the organization and the imposition of related corporate processes such as project approval, project steering, governance and talent management. This is top down in nature and forces compliance with process because it is a mark of good management discipline. It assumes that a focus upon the competencies of project management will follow, as a means to support the newly established disciplines and probably in response to further senior management pressure.

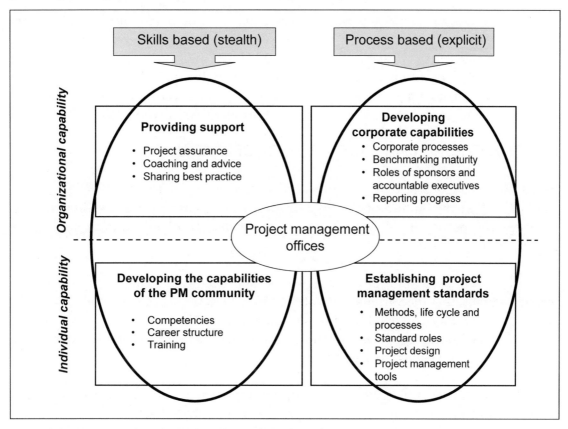

Figure 3.8   Implementing a framework

STEALTHY CHANGE

The alternative, stealthier route in Figure 3.8 is based upon the definition of project management competencies, actions to build these competencies within staff and the provision of an expert coaching service to help project staff improve their performance as quickly as possible. This is bottom up and relies on careful and visible demonstration of the resultant improvements. We want to gradually alert senior management that 'something right is going on over there'. The approach assumes that a focus on project management disciplines will then follow, as senior management see this as a way to spread the newly established competency more widely across the organization.

The reader will note that each of these options is a blend of building individual capability and organizational capability and in my experience the two have to progress in parallel. The alternatives do not work in practice:

- Concentrating solely on organizational capabilities (support and organizational processes) is like building upon poor foundations as the underlying, raw materials for project delivery are not in place. It has limited impact on project performance and creates the view of project management disciplines as bureaucracy.

- Concentrating solely on individual capabilities (the competencies of individual project staff and the methodologies of project management to guide them) creates a perception of project management as some dark, unique skill. Again there is the danger of project management being perceived as a complex bureaucracy, disconnected from BAU. It might demonstrate improved project performance in terms of solution delivery, but without supportive organizational processes that will approve and govern projects responsibly it is probable that projects will still fail to deliver improved business benefits.

ROADMAPS FOR IMPROVING PROJECT DELIVERY

As for any change project, the approach adopted to improve project delivery must carefully reflect the culture of the organization and its current business imperatives. So, there can be no single, best answer to the challenge of introducing sustainable improvements.

What is important, in order to make the improvements sustainable, is that they build gradually, that the various parts of the framework reinforce one another and that each new capability is embedded into the organization. Just like any project, it pays to have a plan, to manage how the various initiatives complement one another and to demonstrate improvement to stakeholders.

Figures 3.9 and 3.10 depict two alternative approaches, one initially led by process (explicit) and one initially led by competencies (stealthy). Each of them produces deliverables that map to the model characteristics of companies that excel in project delivery (see page 33).

Figure 3.9's roadmap starts with a very visible deployment of a project management methodology. This will require some form of direct instruction from the highest levels of the organization (perhaps as a reaction to some severe problem or failure of a critical project) and will require some parallel adjustment to corporate processes for project approval to force compliance with the new methodology. There will be new, high-profile projects starting and the new methodology will be imposed upon them.

As a public message of the new way of working, there is an early move to form project offices in business divisions or at head office and these project offices initially focus on monitoring project progress (to advise senior management of the improvements that are resulting from the new project management processes).

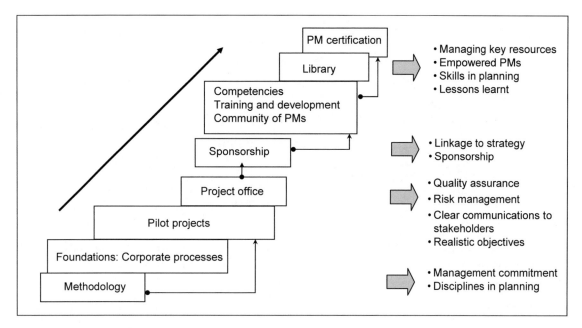

Figure 3.9   Roadmap initiated by process

When this focus on project management disciplines uncovers the true risks in the projects, many of which will be related to the skills and experience of project staff, the organization's attention will turn to improving the required skills. Training, coaching and the re-use of good practice will be initiated. The organization's focus on formality will lead it to adopt some form of independent certification of project managers and this certification will be used to select capable project managers for major projects.

Figure 3.10 shows the more stealthy approach, where the starting point is to practically support some critical projects through a coaching service and to work with the internal training function to design a training curriculum that will cover project management skills. There will be limited interest in project management certification in the early days.

A central team or a peer group approach will be needed to start this improvement process. Part of their role is to publicize successes in the organization and as these start to be recognized, the roadmap moves into process-related areas, building a project management methodology and a library to share best practice. A key step in this roadmap is to introduce the concept of two-stage projects (see later) and this is used to start engaging senior management, to be followed by education for senior managers in the art of sponsoring projects.

The platform provided by initial work on project methods then leads the improvement programme into a broader effort to improve other corporate processes related to projects, supported by the formation of project offices in each business area. The project offices will initially be focused on quality assurance, best practice and the allocation of scarce project resources, but will later track project progress.

The final area addressed in this improvement programme is to work with sponsors and accountable executives on how they form and structure projects; this process

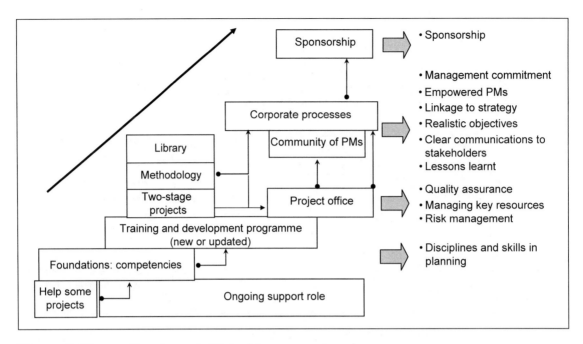

Figure 3.10   Roadmap initiated by competencies

requires a combination of good project management practice and engagement of senior line managers to address the critical, early stages of the projects (and this is an entry point to a future debate about the linkage between business strategy and projects).

For any organization, the precise approach will vary. In these two examples, the roles of project offices were initially completely different: one focused on tracking project progress and the other focused on best practice and resource allocation. These change programmes to improve project performance must be alert to business imperatives and priorities and be opportunistic by adjusting the programme of work and key messages to take advantage of new developments.

Having discussed some alternative roadmaps for change, let us examine some ways in which we can ensure that management support is maintained through the process.

GETTING MANAGEMENT ATTENTION

Symbols and messages

Whatever the roadmap, one needs to gain the attention of senior management. This might be easier with an explicit change approach that has top-down direction, but even in this case we need some way to help management visualize the challenges of delivering projects.

There are various ways of demonstrating visible success or a clear portrayal of project management's unique contribution to the organization, their value depending on the situation in which the organization finds itself. Here are some examples:

- Find a critical project for a big win. If the organization has a project underway that is recognized as business critical, find a way to introduce better project management disciplines, resourcing or sponsorship so that the project delivers to plan. Year 2000 was a great example of such a project. Other high-profile projects are acquisition integrations and brand launches.

- Use a critical challenge that the organization faces as the host for project management. Tailor the sales messages to reflect this challenge. It could be time-to-market, or agility in the face of a volatile business climate. In financial services today, where the overhead of demonstrating regulatory compliance is growing fast, perhaps the discipline of project management can be deployed to reduce the size of the task. Most companies today have more strategic opportunities than they have resources, so it might be useful to depict the benefits of project management more as the ability to make better use of scarce resources (the opportunity cost/ profit argument) and less as the ability to reduce costs on project delivery.

- Find a way to significantly improve the visibility of project performance, as described earlier in this chapter, so that senior managers are better informed of progress and issues. The introduction of balanced scorecards is one technique, as is a RAG traffic light system of indicating project health.

- Find a project where vendor management is complex and where progress is patchy. Apply experienced project and commercial skills to improve the situation. Most project managers in BAU organizations have more limited commercial skills than those in projectized organizations. Often the project managers have moved into project management from the technology function, with limited experience on managing contracts, or they have been line managers who have used vendors in an ongoing BAU context, not the delivery of solutions within a project life cycle. Applying professional disciplines here can make a noticeable, profitable difference.

- Rather than trying to engage senior managers with a description of the complexities of project management, find a single, symbolic message that distils the central challenge that the organization has to tackle, then repeat that message continually until it starts to make an impression; this is change management by repetition! Here are two examples, one conceptual and one practical.

In BAU life, every day brings opportunities to fine-tune processes and operations. BAU managers engage on regular, incremental improvements (just like fine-tuning the speed and workflow in an assembly production line). In a project, with a defined goal and timescale, we make key decisions early on about how the project will progress. After these decisions are made, our ability to influence the outcome of the project steadily reduces. We can of course still affect the outcome, and poor execution can still cause failure, but by the time a project is through its design stages we have set its course and fate. If we wish to revisit these decisions then the whole project goes back to the drawing board. This is a key difference between BAU and project work.

Figure 3.11 highlights this fundamental difference. The point for senior management is that this one diagram drives the need for special techniques and skills in a project:

- why we talk about a project having a life cycle;

- why designing the project structure and team carefully is so important and why the structure might change during the life cycle;

- why key control processes are so critical, as they provide stability of approach through the changing life cycle;

- why sponsor involvement is so important during the early design stages (sponsors cannot just approve the project and then disengage until the project is ready for operational use);

- why late changes are so serious to project progress.

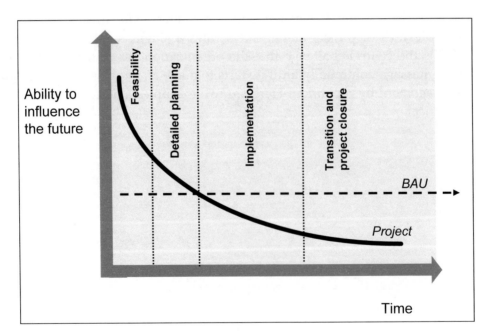

Figure 3.11   Why projects are different

This one diagram is why projects are not the same as BAU. This might be a slightly simplistic view of the world, but it makes a powerful point and does it without forcing senior managers to get into the details of project management techniques.

A common problem in BAU organizations is a poor appreciation of how risk and uncertainty manifest themselves in a project. Estimates made in the early stages of a project are subject to high uncertainty (a fact recognized in projectized companies where principles of estimating error and allocation of contingencies are long established and the subject of much academic research). BAU organizations often fail to appreciate this and assume that the initial estimates are accurate.

This attitude can result in projects submitting themselves for approval just once, for the whole project, and then not returning for formal approval again (at least, not until they realize that they need more funding and have to return for approval, an experience that is unpleasant because it is a surprise to the project sponsor).

The danger of optimistic estimates can become increased because BAU budget processes and deadlines can force project teams to rush their initial estimating work or do it before they have sufficient information.

The impact of this problem is wider than the potential failure of a particular project. Having underestimated the scale of each project, the organization then takes on too many projects, which leads to an increased demand for scarce project and business skills. These stretched resources then allow insufficient time for planning and the vicious cycle starts all over again.

Projectized organizations realize this and regularly revisit the estimates of cost, resource and time. Complex projects are delivered as a series of stages to reduce risk. A first step to introducing a staged approach into a BAU organization is to institute a formal re-approval of each project at the end of its planning stage, when estimates can be expected to have improved in accuracy. We can sell this to senior management as an opportunity for them to influence events (always a good sales pitch to managers) and make the point that it will reduce time-to-market for the projects, since rework is the biggest cause of project delays. See Figure 3.12.

We need a simple message for this approach. I have used 'two-stage projects' as a strapline as it gets the message across and implies simplicity.

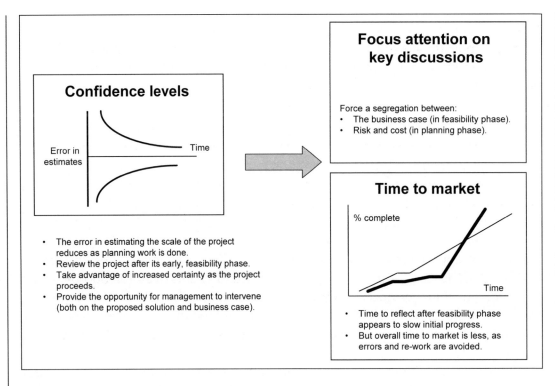

Figure 3.12   Two-stage projects

In reality the process gets more complex and, as we shall see later in Chapters 4 and 5, there is a need in today's volatile world for projects to be delivered in even shorter stages. As a first step, moving to two-stage projects sends a powerful signal to the organization.

Designing the project's structure

This skill is worthy of specific mention in the context of gaining management attention.

As described earlier, this is a key skill for project managers, but is not well appreciated by BAU organizations. Why should they, when they do not really appreciate the uniqueness of a project life cycle?

The sales message required to awake the organization to this skill will vary. It could be based upon either of the concepts in the two panels above; as a way of helping senior management to influence the project in its early stages or as a logical part of the review within a two-stage project. It could be raised as a response to a failed project where organizational problems were the root causes of failure.

The recognition within the organization of this skill can create management support for several parts of the framework. It can lead to the formation of a centre of best practice and enforce their engagement on projects at the early, most critical stages. It can be a means to ensure that project teams have the required skills and experience. It can be used to set out the ongoing governance and assurance that the project should receive.

Things to avoid

When introducing project management, we must be careful to avoid, in our zeal, pushing approaches that will never really take hold in the organization. There are, in effect, some areas where we should compromise from an ideal model of project management.

This might be heresy to some readers, but some aspects of project management will have limited appeal. Post implementation reviews would be one example; for all the advantages of using such reviews as a way of learning lessons, they are very difficult approaches to embed within BAU organizations. BAU organizations just find it hard to apply this discipline, unlike projectized organizations where it is an integral part of how they operate. Some consulting organizations, for example, will not reward teams for a project until they have lodged new intellectual capital into the corporate library.

In defense of BAU organizations, they do have the challenge of moving staff back to BAU and they do have to face the low repeatability between projects, which will limit the value of a post implementation review. So such reviews must be more concise than one would see in a projectized organization.

Project management methodologies and tools have to reflect the culture of the organization. If either is too complex or bureaucratic, then they will not be applied. The key fact to remember is that BAU change projects are not usually that complex in a logistical sense, unlike building a petrochemical plant or launching a space shuttle where the scheduling of tasks, dependencies and large numbers of resources are the focus of project control. The key challenges in change projects are usually the engagement of stakeholders and the scheduling of a few key resources such as business users, technology experts or solution architects. These experts are individuals, not a commodity; can we do this project twice as fast with twice the resources, just as we accelerate a building project by doubling the number of bricklayers or plasterers? Not usually! The tools and methodologies that you select must be appropriate to the needs of the organization.

MOVING ON THE AGENDA

As in any change programme, the leader of the project improvement programme must be looking to keep the agenda fresh. Organizations have short memories and last year's success will be discounted if it is not followed by further gains. When a project improvement programme first starts, the results are best measured simply and the classic choices will be the schedule and cost performance of the projects. What percentage late or over budget were projects before the programme started and what percentage late and over budget are they now? If this measure can be used effectively it is a great communication message and can be compared with much published research on project performance.

There are several problems with this measure though. The first is due to the low repeatability of projects in BAU organizations. Unless one can average the performance across a large population of projects, the unique nature of each project will result in unpredictable results that will not necessarily demonstrate the added value of introducing project management disciplines.

A further problem is that the application of project management disciplines often makes the apparent performance of projects deteriorate. Problems such as over-runs on cost or unrealistic timelines that were hidden before through poor control or reporting will surface because of the more rigorous approach.

Even if the organization does not suffer these problems, these simple measures of improvement are quite short lived. After a while, as projects are planned and estimated better, their performance gets closer to budget, so the percentage improvement reduces.

At this point, the improvement programme needs to change the measure of success. The next measure could be of predictability – variations from estimates. This is a message that plays well with senior executives who, just like anyone, hate surprises. So, predictability is a good measure politically and a realistic assessment of how project management disciplines are improving the practice of delivering projects.

All of the above measures, though, are focused on the delivery of the project's solution, only one of the three key elements that we discussed earlier – what about change management and benefits?

There is an issue of maturity here. The impact of change is hard to quantify and harder to compare across projects. We also cannot start our improvement programme with project benefits as a measure of success because this requires the organization to measure benefits in a structured manner and this is unlikely to be possible in the early stages of a project improvement programme.

As our approach to delivering projects matures, though, we can start to consider how we move on to use benefits as the measure of project success. There are various types of benefits, but the most practical measure to start with is the tangible, financial benefits which are the core of the business case of most projects. Some will have to be estimated (for example, it might be difficult to differentiate between business growth due to a project and that due to some BAU improvement) but this should not affect the value of the measure if sufficient projects are analysed.

It is at this stage that the project management champion in the organization typically starts to talk in terms of programmes, which as we will see in Chapter 4 are management frameworks for the delivery of business benefits.

4 TAKING STOCK – PROGRESS SO FAR, CHALLENGES AHEAD

PROGRESS SO FAR IN BAU ORGANIZATIONS

So far in this chapter, we have looked at the framework of measures that can improve the project management capability of an organization. We have considered the techniques of managing the project solution, managing change and managing benefits, and considered how these can be improved through a combination of:

- competencies for project management, supported by education;
- standards for the project life cycle and key project management processes;
- supportive corporate processes, including governance;
- educated sponsors;
- managing project resources with care;
- coaching and assurance.

While I hope that my depiction of the framework is clear and useful, the individual elements of the framework will not be news to most project managers or champions of project management. Prior to the 1990s, many companies had made the mistake of thinking that they could fix their project management problems with just one of these elements, but in recent years organizations have realized that a balanced set of these measures is the key to sustainable improvement in the performance of delivering projects.

In projectized organizations, there is much historical data to show how these measures have improved project management performance. Of course, in projectized organizations it is quite easy to get senior management to appreciate the value of such approaches but in BAU organizations there is a more limited appreciation of the issues and of the attention required.

However, we can see that such measures make a difference in BAU organizations as well. In my recent experience in a bank, focusing on the standards for project management, training, improved governance and providing a coaching service for project managers resulted in a 15 per cent improvement in project performance (calculated in terms of both schedule and cost performance). Today, many BAU organizations have started to demonstrate similar savings.

BAU organizations typically find it easier to make progress on the parts of the framework that are based upon techniques (standards, and so on) rather than on the people aspects of project management. In a recent benchmarking exercise that I carried out with 12 financial services companies, I found that most of them had made encouraging progress with the implementation of:

- a standard project life cycle (or at least just a few variants)

- standardized project management processes

- recognition of business owners/accountable executives

- a focus on the demands of sponsorship

- emerging concepts of benefits realization.

Most banks had project management offices established (either to monitor project progress or to act as centres of excellence, occasionally as both). Most were taking the early steps in assessing the overall portfolio of projects, to improve the linkage of projects to business strategy.

The areas where the framework was lagging were the people aspects of project management. These were typically described as:

- how we ensure that the project team has adequate project management skills;

- how we structure projects in a way that recognizes the needs of the project, the available skills and the demands of the organization;

- how we drive better change management and benefits realization, where techniques are less defined than those for solution delivery;

- how we re-integrate staff and knowledge back into the business.

The overwhelming view of the organizations that I interviewed was that the basic project management techniques and processes are now in place and these issues of 'human capital' were now key to making further improvements in project performance.

OPTIONS FOR PROVIDING PROJECT DELIVERY SKILLS

What are the models that BAU organizations use to allocate resources who are experienced in project management, change and benefits realization to their change projects? How do they structure projects in a considered manner? How do they re-integrate project staff back into the organization?

Some organizations have taken the step of gathering together all their project management resources into a central pool or a small number of central pools. This is the 'projects division' approach and is a quite natural path for organizations that want to seriously address their skills issues in project delivery. It gives critical mass and a coherent skills family and facilitates coaching, career development and the retention and reuse of good practice – all built upon the framework described earlier in this chapter. It allows experts to contribute to the design of project structures.

This approach is most common in organizations that are operating in a single or few countries, where the management of a central pool is more feasible.

Some organizations have taken this 'skills pool' concept but applied it at a more local level, typically at a country level if the organization is international or at a business division level. Such teams are often called 'change delivery' or 'business change'. As the pools are located in various parts of the organization, skills families that span across the enterprise are formed to encourage knowledge sharing and common standards.

Finally, some organizations do not have such pools at all, but allocate BAU staff to projects within each part of the organization.

Note that these relatively few options for how resources are applied to projects are really trading off project management expertise against domain expertise and proximity to the business. Other more complex models, usually based on some form of matrix management that balances skills sets, projects and business areas, are more prevalent in projectized organizations but it is the simpler debates of how centralized the resources should be and how dedicated they are to project work that are most relevant in BAU organizations.

For clarity, this is not exclusively the case and some other models are used within certain discrete areas of the business. For example, technology functions will often use a matrix structure so that they can build teams of mixed skills (architects, software developers, infrastructure technicians, networking specialists, testers) and apply them to business projects and ongoing application support. In a way, this proves the difference between BAU and projectized organizations, for the technology function is really a projectized organization residing within the BAU organization; it manages a steady stream of projects, so invests in the skills, organizational models and reuse of good practice that is typical for a projectized organization. It is also why the technology function is often the source of project management resources for the business and often the starting point for initiatives to improve project management across the organization.

	Projects division	Pools/skills family	Dispersed
Efficiency			
Costs	+ Economies of scale − But a visible cost	− Limited economies of scale Visible only in business unit	− High unit cost Costs are dispersed
Flexibility	+ Portfolio effect helps − Still limited cross business	+ Good within business unit	− Limited capacity
Responsiveness	− Needs engagement process	+ Good within business unit	+ Fast reaction
Effectiveness			
The right team	+ Good process skills − Issue with business skills	Blend of process/business	+ Good business skills − Issue with allocation to project
The right solution	Right solution for organization	Right solution for the business unit	Point solution
The right results	− Issues with change management	+ Likely best outcome	+ Best potential benefits − Issues with execution

Figure 3.13   Providing human capital

Figure 3.13 compares the three options for staffing projects. One trades off the discipline and experience of the project process (which might make the delivery of the solution more efficient but will increase the risk of change management problems) with local business knowledge and contacts (which might help the projects to be effective in delivering change but will increase the risk of problems in the project process).

Let's take this theme of a centralized skill set versus a skill set that is dispersed in the business a bit further. To start with, let's consider the skill of project delivery as a spectrum, at one end of which the skills are managed as a very discrete skill set and at the other end of which they are managed as a skill set that is dispersed and embedded within the organization.

Companies have typically started with an embedded but ill-defined skill set. They have neither a clear methodology for the delivery of projects nor a concept of a discrete set of skills required to deliver projects. They find that they have problems in delivering projects successfully and embark upon the implementation of a project management framework. As described earlier in this chapter, such a framework produces an improvement and this improvement happens first and fastest in the more technique-oriented parts of the framework: methodology, project management disciplines, training in basic project management skills, clearer roles on projects, reuse of good practice.

Some organizations have carried on down this increasingly specialized and discrete route, progressing through local pools of staff who are primarily focused on project work and some have progressed as far as the segregated projects division.

The progression is quite natural, particularly where the skill set is being directed by leaders who have entered their roles from technology functions or from other organizations that are more projectized in nature. Members of the project management profession have a natural inclination for the discipline, consistency and robustness of the segregated model and a natural desire to nurture the project management skills of the organization. We also know that previous experience on projects is one of the best predictors of project success!

However, I contend that this very specialized model of providing the human capital to business change projects will not prove successful in the long term. Quite simply, the efficiency advantages of discipline, consistency and reuse will tend to be more than negated by the problems that come from such a model:

- A typical BAU organization does not have the same repeatability of projects as a typical projectized organization. A systems integrator might roll out a large number of similar projects (take enterprise packaged applications for finance, human resource management, logistics or manufacturing as examples) but a typical BAU organization does not obtain the same benefits of concentrating staff to reuse knowledge and make future projects easier.

- Business change projects require significant management of stakeholders. If the project team are from outside their area, stakeholders are inevitably harder to manage and prone to assume that the project is 'being done to us' by 'them'.

- Because 'them' is a group from elsewhere in the organization, there is also a tendency for the stakeholders to categorize them as not understanding the issues or just simply as being incapable of the role.

The limited reuse also means that it is much harder to obtain high utilization of specialized project staff, so the projects division ends up being a significant cost that the organization can regard as inappropriate.

5 A PROPOSITION

Even those companies that have not progressed very far in building a specialist skill set have started to become concerned that they are building too much of a discrete specialism. This view came out in the benchmarking exercise that I described earlier.

> 'We don't want a specialist skill. We want all of our more senior managers to be able to play their part in managing change as well as managing BAU activity.'
>
> 'We will never obtain the recognition that projects are a part of BAU activity if we keep promoting it as a unique, special skill.'

This concern embraces the fact that many business change projects will be led or staffed by occasional project members, not by specialists or project management professionals. Why? Because in many cases that is the most effective way of staffing projects and because the project team members are close to the needs of the business and respected by other stakeholders within the business. Their project management skills might be less developed than those of professional, regular project managers but their BAU knowledge and position equip them to deliver change more effectively.

If we can provide these occasional project members with assistance on project management disciplines and techniques, in a way that is sensitive to their backgrounds, perhaps we can get the best of both worlds in terms of project success.

This theme of embedding the skill of project management more deeply in the organization matches with the desire to help all employees to become more change aware: to bring the competencies of change inside BAU, as just another part of the toolkit of techniques that any team leader or manager needs, not as a skill that is regarded a special and outside BAU.

In analysis within an international bank, approaching 80 per cent of project managers were seconded line managers (and therefore not a part of the recognized project management skills family).

Half of these seconded line managers were still undertaking a BAU role while managing the project.

Of these seconded line managers 45 per cent had not received any formal project management training (being outside the target audience for such training).

Of course, we are not going to be able to remove the specialist skill set entirely. First of all, some areas such as technology or product development will need more of a specialized skill set. In addition, we have to create some centre of project expertise, or we will not be able to provide assistance to all those project staff who have been seconded from BAU roles, assistance that will become more critical on the more complex projects. Figure 3.14 depicts this strategy.

I propose that BAU organizations now have two parallel challenges to face if they are to continue to improve the success rate of change projects. They should turn their attention to better embedding the project management skill set within a broad range of people in the organization – 'occasional project managers and teams'. They will still need to build their specialist project management skills, but this work should be concentrated on localized areas and 'regular project managers' where a more projectized approach is appropriate.

There are therefore two communities of project staff to address within the organization; two communities to inform, educate, develop and support in two different ways.

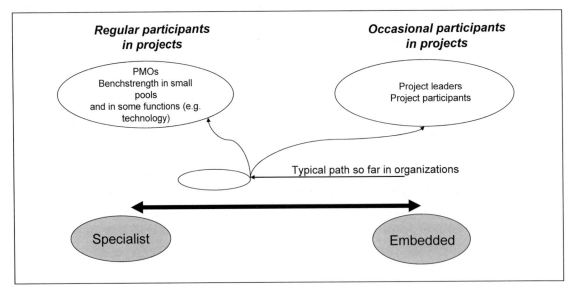

Figure 3.14   Two communities who deliver projects

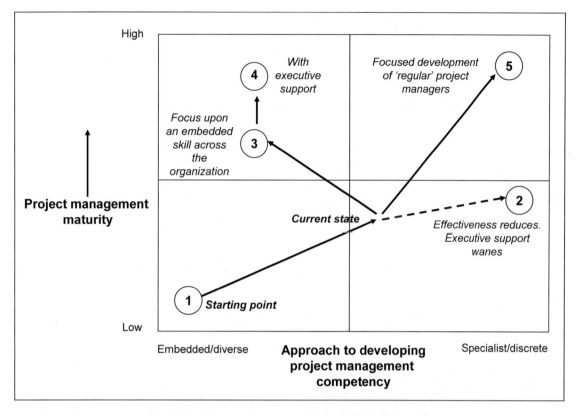

Figure 3.15   Impact of the embedded model on maturity

Figure 3.15 encapsulates how this strategy can help organizations to keep improving their project management maturity and project delivery performance.

- Most organizations started with a skill set that was embedded – but with such limited focus and such an immature approach that project performance was poor (point 1).

- Organizations have invested in project management frameworks to improve their performance and results have been encouraging (the 15 to 20 per cent improvement cited earlier).

- But these improvements suffer from diminishing returns as organizations try to move towards more specialized models. Project efficiency and performance still improves, albeit at a lesser rate, but the change management effectiveness of the organization is hampered by the specialist nature of the skill; in addition, the organization starts to view project management as a specialized, costly bureaucracy and executive support for the discipline wanes (point 2).

- If we can focus on the needs of the occasional project members, with support and techniques that feel more like BAU, then it is my assertion that this will produce further improvements in project performance for those many BAU organizations who have already invested in project management frameworks (point 3).

- The right techniques and skills, well presented to this broader community, will on their own improve performance. They will also help us to depict the discipline of project management to executives in a more acceptable way (less of an overhead, more as an enabler of change) and this will gain executive support for the approach, further enhancing maturity and performance (point 4).

- In parallel, we can keep working on the skills of our regular, professional project managers. They can receive development that is tailored to their needs, not diluted by the needs of the occasional project members, which should allow their own maturity to increase faster (point 5).

Where campaigns to improve project delivery in BAU organizations are losing momentum, this strategy offers a means to re-energize the efforts.

6 AN EMBEDDED FRAMEWORK FOR PROJECT DELIVERY

An embedded model of providing the skills for delivering projects would:

- provide project teams with a more subtle set of approaches that feels less specialized;

- focus on using specialists as a coaching or support service rather than to lead projects;

- let the business take responsibility for the improvements in project delivery performance from within, rather than proving the value of the project management discipline as a separate exercise.

What would this more subtle approach to developing a project management framework look like? This section takes some key parts of the framework in turn and discusses the impact of the embedded approach. This is summarized in Figures 3.16 and 3.17.

THE CAPABILITIES OF THE PROJECT MANAGEMENT COMMUNITY

Project management career path

We now have two career paths related to project management. We still need a formal career path for those regular project managers who see their career developing within the project management 'skills family', a career path that would include professional recognition at key points through the educational and experience requirements of professional associations such as the Association for Project Management or Project Management Institute.

For occasional project managers and project staff, the organization's generic approach to career development should be modified to recognize that there are particular skills that individuals will pick up during project work that will enhance their progression in their own skills family. Examples would be:

- setting clear business goals;

- leading change;

- managing uncertainty.

This approach is a reflection of the embedded strategy, but also helps to promote project delivery as a valuable addition to the skill set of any individual.

Training

Similarly, we should have two curricula for the training of project management staff. The curriculum for regular project managers will be as described earlier in this chapter – a progression from the basic techniques of project management through to the softer skills and complexities of leading teams through change. We should make sure that this training curriculum, like the project management skill family, gets recognized in the talent management process for the organization but we should not try to force occasional project managers into it.

There should be a second curriculum for occasional project resources and this curriculum has two aspects. The visible aspect should be a curriculum that demonstrates the key practices and techniques of project management in a concise manner (project management 'lite'). Such training is widely available today in varied formats including e-learning, simulations and classroom training. The design of the training should allow it to be delivered 'just-in-time' when a project team is being formed and the skills can be immediately applied on a live project. On complex projects, such training can be given as a facilitated workshop, where an external consultant helps the project team to develop the scope and action plan for the project and debate potential risks and conflicts. Again, such events are widely available.

The process used to approve and fund new projects must account for such training – mandating its use and forcing the inclusion of the related costs in the project's budget. The costs are insignificant compared with the potential savings or wastage on the project (on a £10 million project a set of start-up facilitated workshops might cost £20 000, a 0.2 per cent investment that could save many times that on the project) but without a forcing mechanism this expense can be seen as profligate or discretionary by those who approve budgets.

The second aspect of the curriculum for occasional project staff is the subtler embedding of key project management techniques or concepts into generic education across the organization:

- Concepts of project finance and benefits realization could be embedded within existing courses for financial control or the appraisal of investments.

- Basic project management techniques could be embedded into training for team leading for first-line supervisors or into courses on setting goals and managing work.

- Existing workshops or events that build leadership skills could include structured approaches to managing change and the concepts of project sponsorship.

- Training on operational risk (a key focus these days for financial and other institutions) could include the techniques used for managing risks on projects.

- The technique of carefully structuring a project to meet the needs of the work and organizational breakdown structures could be included within existing courses that cover BAU organizational design.

Human resources focus

In a projectized environment, the focus of the human resources function is to ensure that there is a career path for project specialists and that there is a clear strategy for the provision of project resources to projects. In the embedded model, the focus is much more about how BAU staff are allocated to projects, how their own career development can benefit from the assignment, how their career interests are protected while they are seconded to a project and how they are re-integrated back into a BAU role thereafter. Managing the reward process such that it fairly reflects their contribution to the project will be another area of focus.

These areas cause many problems in BAU organizations; since the project is a temporary organization, it is easy for this lack of continuity to mean that the contribution, reward and re-integration of seconded staff are handled badly. We should focus the organization on these areas and develop approaches that will improve performance, examples being:

- using 'career anchors', BAU managers who will keep in contact with staff while they are allocated to projects and be jointly responsible with the project manager to agree a plan for the re-integration of staff back to BAU roles;

- adjusting the reward scheme to ensure that project contributions are recognized (the use of bonus payments based upon achieving key project milestones, ensuring that there is continuity of salary levels, and so on);

- public recognition of the efforts of the project team in a similar manner to how BAU teams are recognized.

Source of project resources

In the embedded model, we recognize that project resources will be acquired primarily from the business to maximize business knowledge, commitment and buy-in from other stakeholders.

Specialists will be used where there is a projectized culture in a part of the organization (technology or a shared service centre). In addition, the organization will also need a relatively small number of experienced project managers to help manage the more major projects and programmes. Since BAU organizations find it difficult to justify the cost of maintaining these expensive resources, they should be gathered together in a skills family (not pool) so that utilization levels can be maximized.

An alternative is to source experienced project and programme managers externally, only when needed. This has always been a recognized source of such skills, but the track record of external project managers succeeding on business change projects is patchy because of their lack of specific business knowledge and poor awareness of political and organizational issues in the organization. In the embedded approach, the crucial difference is that a seconded BAU manager will be the formal, visible leader of the project. The experienced project management resources are more likely to be supporting that leader with project management expertise and the disciplines that will allow the project to deliver as planned. This hybrid team of 'project director and project manager' has worked extremely well in my experience. It provides a good blend of business leadership and project management skill.

ESTABLISHING PROJECT MANAGEMENT STANDARDS

Methods and standards

Traditional project management methodologies can look very complex and technical to BAU personnel. They are also very focused upon the delivery of the project solution rather than the broader issues of change management and benefits realization. Our profession has paid some attention to the challenge of reducing this complexity, particularly when addressing the delivery of small projects. However, project methodologies in a BAU organization need to appear simple even for very large projects.

The methodology described in Appendix 1 has been designed to appeal to BAU staff who are working on projects. It is really a set of minimum standards. It distils the project into nine processes (as per Figure 3.5 earlier) and as the project moves through its life cycle of five stages, it is relatively simple to depict the key tasks in each stage that should result in good discipline.

Those who champion project management in BAU organizations should keep emphasizing the simple processes and the life cycle. The methodology could be depicted more as a set of workbooks that would help project staff to ensure that they had included all required tasks in their plans and in their estimates of costs and timescales.

Later in this book I will discuss some of the barriers to introducing benefits management into BAU organizations. While leaving the details of the subject until later, it is worthy of note here that if we position the disciplines of benefits management in an embedded way, linked to BAU processes for financial management, there is a greater chance of their being accepted than if we present them as a specialist discipline. The same logic applies to change management.

Tool support

Traditional project management tools based upon critical-path networking and work/organization breakdown structures still have their place, particularly for the professional project managers and PMOs who will help to control the more complex projects and programmes. For most projects, where the challenges are more to do with change than the control of complex logistics, we should use tools that promote collaboration and the simple depiction of work (task lists and milestone lists for example, rather than Gantt charts).

	Project community	BAU community
Career development	• Formal career path, certification	• Skills that complement other career paths
Training	• Traditional progress through techniques and soft/leadership skills	• PM 'lite', just in time delivery, embed PM skills into the corporate curriculum
Focus of HR	• Career development of specialists • Resource strategy	• Allocation, care and re-integration of seconded staff
Source of project resources	• Skills pools in specific areas (e.g. IT) and of specialists for support to complex projects	• BAU functions. Support via specialists or PMOs
Methods and standards	• Robust PM methods	• Minimum standards and control processes

Figure 3.16   Project management framework for two communities (1)

DEVELOPING CORPORATE CAPABILITIES

Governance of projects

If we follow again the logic of making our approaches feel more like BAU, how might we alter the formal steering of projects, through discrete committees, that is the norm in projectized organizations? We still need a way of engaging various stakeholders in formal governance of the project, but many of these stakeholders will be members of the management team that is affected by the project. With an embedded approach, we might include the steering of key projects within the agenda of a meeting that already takes place; a management meeting that already monitors business growth and performance would be appropriate. This has the advantage of building very visible, collective support for the project.

One risk of this embedded approach is that this less obvious governance results in superficial coverage of projects or that projects are assessed very much in isolation, so that the relative benefits of each project investment are never considered. Mitigating this risk requires the technique of portfolio management, which we will discuss in detail in Chapter 5.

PROVIDING SUPPORT

Quality assurance and the role of the PMO

In our traditional project management framework, we provided some form of independent review of progress and quality, through a standardized review (healthcheck) that might be conducted by a peer project manager or PMO. A PMO also monitored project progress, and the discipline of formal funding reviews of the project at the end of each stage adds to the level of assurance.

In the embedded model, the PMOs can act as clearing houses to arrange independent reviews but the organization will inevitably find it harder to do this as projects will be less visible across the enterprise.

We should recognize, though, that the close engagement of stakeholders who will inherit the results and benefits of the project is a powerful driver for good performance, and a driver that is not present in most projectized organizations. In addition, the use of formal presentations of project progress at stage transitions/tollgates will provide a regular review that is more in tune with BAU business review processes.

As a further layer of assurance, the embedded model could also rely on the use of the internal audit function. In many BAU organizations, and definitely in financial services companies, there is a strong internal audit function present to ensure compliance with good business practices and legal obligations. The audit function will typically look at significant projects since they introduce risk to the organization. If they are provided with a set of questions based upon the minimum standards for project management, they can review the health of projects in an informed manner.

Project tracking, on the embedded model, could be allocated to an appropriate BAU function, which in most financial services companies would be finance. They will need some standardized means to receive project progress information and some education so that they can interpret progress statements correctly.

In BAU organizations, where finance functions are experienced in monitoring BAU activity that has a reasonably constant run rate during the year, they usually will require education on project finance issues.

Finance has a tendency to look at cost information without considering time and scope. A project that has spent less than planned is assumed to be in good health, whereas in reality it could simply be running late...and over budget, not under!

Promoting reuse of good practice

The role of the PMO is critical to the reuse of good practice within the embedded model, since there is little prospect of this being achieved automatically within BAU functions, even if some form of knowledge management system or project library is provided. These approaches work in projectized organizations because their importance is recognized and institutionalized but are unlikely to happen in a BAU organization under the embedded model, unless they are included in the minimum standards and the PMO prompts for them to happen.

	Project community	BAU community
Tools	• Traditional PM tools, knowledge management	• Collaboration, workflow, presentation
Project governance	• Formal PSCs • PMO for tracking	• Embed in scheduled meetings • Finance/strategy processes
Quality assurance	• Peer and PMO reviews • PMO tracking • Formal stage reviews	• Peer review • Audit/independent review • Stage reviews
Focus of the PMO	• Tracking projects • Quality assurance • Allocating resources • Centre of expertise • Portfolio management	• Done by BAU functions • Focus on start-up service • Only for specialist support • Centre of expertise • Done by BAU functions
Re-use of good practice	• Knowledge system • Post implementation review	• PMO • Library

Figure 3.17   Project management framework for two communities (2)

7 CONCLUSION – A CASE FOR HUMILITY?

In this chapter we have considered the three stages of project delivery – solution delivery, change management and benefits realization. We have discussed a project management framework that can be used to deliver improved performance in all three areas and which borrows many of its principles from projectized organizations.

Such frameworks have demonstrated their value in many BAU organizations and have proved particularly worthwhile in building the recognition of project management as a discrete discipline with its own unique set of competencies and techniques.

Project management frameworks have had less impact and created less momentum for improvement in the softer, 'human capital' aspects of project delivery. Furthermore, the very visible application of project management disciplines and the specialist nature of project management have resulted in some negative perceptions in BAU organizations. Improvement programmes have slowed and executive support has waned.

How do we build upon the good progress made to date in such organizations and maintain the momentum?

This chapter has proposed that the next stages in improving project delivery have to be subtler, based more upon the embedding of the discipline than on its depiction as a discrete, specialist skill. Many BAU organizations seem to be thinking in this manner, but have not yet moved to formalize and institutionalize this approach.

The approach has significant implications for how project management is portrayed and conducted in BAU organizations. The discipline of project management will have to settle for an apparently lower profile in BAU organizations in return for a better, more visible impact in the long run.

In the next chapters, I will consider how we complement this embedded approach to the skills and techniques of project delivery, by looking at how we embed projects more deeply in the strategic agenda of the organization.

CHAPTER 4

Projects as Agents of Strategic Change – Programme Management

ROADMAP FOR CHAPTER 4

In Chapter 3 we looked at the application of project management disciplines and techniques in BAU organizations. We highlighted how the generic approaches of project management should be tailored as they are applied in BAU organizations for the delivery of projects seeking to change the business. Some of the earlier recommendations reflect simply the nature of 'soft' projects, but many reflect the unique nature of such organizations.

Delivering each and every project to the best of our abilities will certainly be a significant contribution to the performance of the organization. It will ensure that we deliver the benefits we have planned. However, it will not inevitably guarantee that the contribution of each project to the organization's strategic agenda is appropriate or optimal.

This chapter looks at how we can progress, from 'delivering projects right' to 'delivering the right projects'. Our starting point is to consider the volatility and complexity of today's business environment. We will then look at the concept of programme management as a way to address this complexity. The implementation of programme management in BAU organizations has resulted in some notable successes but also suffered from various problems. These will be discussed prior to a description of practical advice on how to make programme management happen. The conclusions of this chapter lead us on to Chapter 5, where the technique of portfolio management is described.

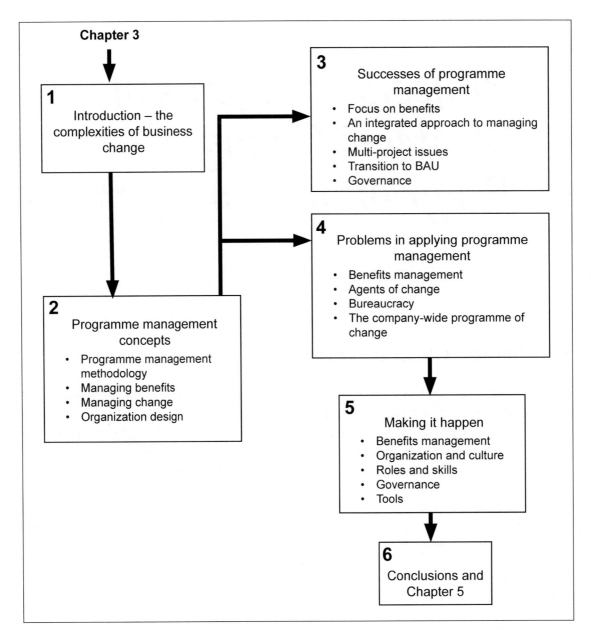

Roadmap for Chapter 4

1 INTRODUCTION – THE COMPLEXITIES OF BUSINESS CHANGE

Given the complexity of today's organizations and a volatile business environment, it is often difficult to provide a clear, well-articulated vision within which the various projects can exist and to which they contribute. Even if a vision is clearly articulated, it can be changed or diluted over time as business needs and market pressures change. In a complex business, the change project can take so long to implement that its duration exceeds the realistic planning horizon of the organization, and changes in business strategy during the delivery period mean that project efforts become less aligned with the goals of the business.

Fewer benefits are eventually delivered from the project. The benefits might even disappear if initial investments prove to be inappropriate for new business needs. In other words, the target that we aimed at when starting the project has moved while we have been delivering it!

This problem with planning horizons is depicted in Figure 4.1. Many enterprise-wide projects suffer from this mismatch between business and project timescales – global product launches, financial management applications, infrastructure projects, research projects, and so on.

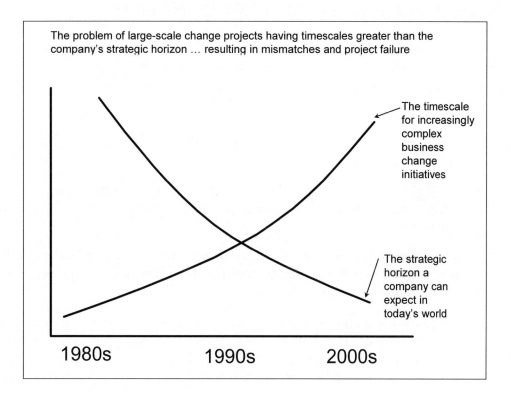

The problem of large-scale change projects having timescales greater than the company's strategic horizon ... resulting in mismatches and project failure

The timescale for increasingly complex business change initiatives

The strategic horizon a company can expect in today's world

1980s   1990s   2000s

Figure 4.1   Planning horizons

Business teams also find it very difficult to appreciate how various projects affect one another. A project might provide a deliverable, such as business capability or information, to another project. Two projects might have a dependency because of the common use of shared resources. If each project is managed in isolation, such issues are not highlighted until a problem occurs.

There are more subtle dependencies between projects when the subject of the project is business change. We discussed the importance of project governance and stakeholder management in Chapter 3. When multiple projects take place in a business, it becomes more difficult to recognize and then manage the expectations of stakeholders. Business managers start to feel that the projects are 'being done to them' as a stream of change initiatives that produces fatigue.

In the absence of an overview of the planned change activities, stakeholders become impatient for results and push project teams to deliver quick wins. I am sure that the reader has experience of the re-engineering or productivity project that seeks early wins ('low hanging fruit', as these are termed) but the early wins are rarely followed by any fundamental or sustainable change.

Business managers are not the only affected parties. Staff in general begin to perceive that there is no overall plan for business change, or journey to a better state, but merely a succession of initiatives.

2 PROGRAMME MANAGEMENT CONCEPTS

Our profession started, in the 1990s, to develop a concept of programme management. Its goal was to find a better way of managing these multiple change projects so that they delivered change and business benefits more effectively. This required an approach that could:

- marshall various related projects so that they were better aligned with the goals of the business;

- recognize that each project delivers some part of an overall programme of change, either some direct benefits or some capability that in turn leads to benefits;

- accommodate changes in the external environment by delivering change incrementally (so if the market changes the effort has still delivered some lasting benefit to the organization);

- give stakeholders a clearer view of the overall change that was being sought.

While there was also an element of controlling the progress of multiple projects (dependencies, shared resource, and so on) the central role of a programme was more focused upon controlling the aggregate change and business benefits of a collection of related projects, in support of some strategic corporate goal. The programme was intended as a bridging layer between corporate strategy and the various change projects. See Figure 4.2.

Defined in this way, a programme is much more than a collection of inter-related projects. It is an organizing or management framework through which inter-related projects deliver business benefits from change projects. The term framework implies that the collection of projects will change if the business needs change; so a programme feels less bounded than a project and should deliver the benefits of change in an iterative fashion.

The concept of evolutionary change leads one to a life cycle for a programme that is iterative rather than a project's closed life cycle. Therefore most commentators have used a description such as depicted in Figure 4.3 where the programme makes progress as a series of cycles, each of which includes the initiation, planning and implementation of various projects. Each cycle is designed to deliver some business benefits in return for the investment that has been made.

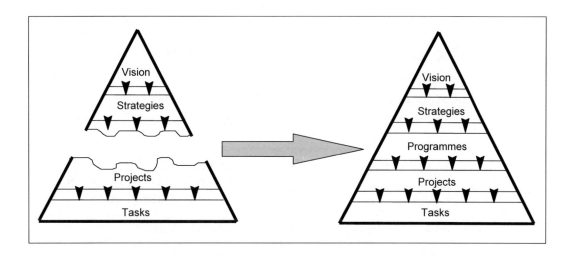

Figure 4.2   The concept of programme management

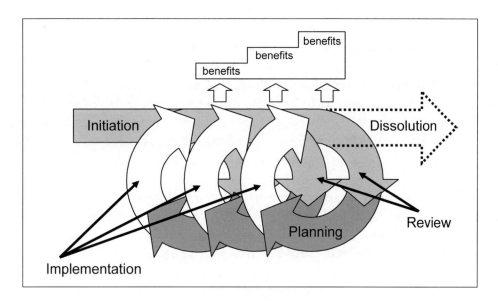

Figure 4.3   The iterative life cycle of a programme

Many definitions of programme management have been coined over the last few years but the sense of a management framework focused upon the benefits of business change is a standard element of the definitions. The Office of Government Commerce publication *Managing Successful Programmes*[1] uses the similar phrase that programme management is 'the coordinated management of a portfolio of projects that change organizations to achieve benefits that are of strategic importance'.

It also helps the understanding of programmes to compare and contrast them with projects. See Figure 4.4.

---

1 *Managing Successful Programmes*, Office of Government Commerce, published by The Stationery Office, 2003, www.tso.co.uk/bookshop.

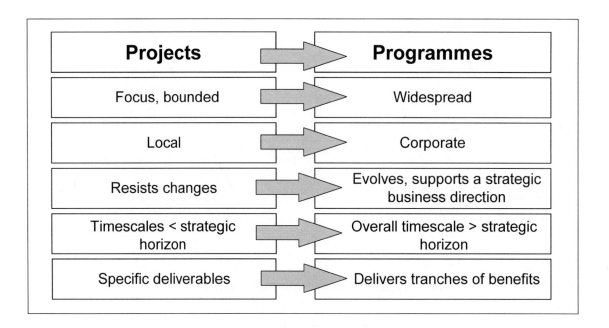

Figure 4.4   How projects and programmes differ

While a project is bounded and follows a closed life cycle of 'design and build', and treats scope changes as risks to be resisted, programmes will evolve as the business needs change and hence will embrace changes in scope rather than resisting them. The programme also dedicates itself to delivering some business benefits in a phased manner rather than a project's focus on a specific set of deliverables.

As Figure 4.5 shows, this difference in character manifests itself in how projects and programmes are controlled – in other words in how project management and programme management are defined. The ownership, approach and focus of management control necessarily differ, as do the deliverables of the exercise.

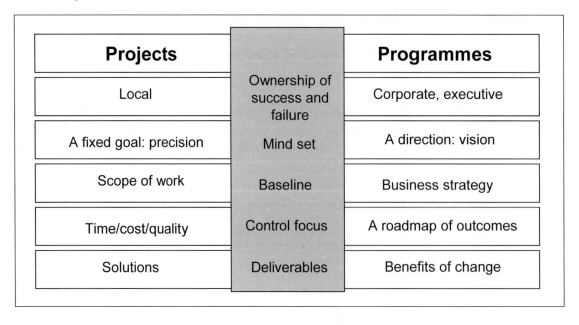

Figure 4.5   Project and programme management

The programme regularly reviews the mix of projects that is being used to address a strategic goal. This helps the organization to prioritize projects by their benefits and contribution to strategic goals. It should also help the organization to coordinate the various changes that result from projects. In order to emphasize this advantage of programme management, we have often used the catchphrase 'project management is about doing projects right but programme management is about doing the right projects'.

PROGRAMME MANAGEMENT METHODOLOGY

In Chapter 3 we discussed a methodology for project management. It was based upon nine processes, operating within a standard life cycle and with standard responsibilities for the key roles on the project.

The core parts of the project management methodology will also apply to a programme. What differs is the more strategic nature of the change, the complexity of managing a collection of related projects and the way in which the processes are used to improve the coordination, strategic alignment and change management of that collection of related projects.

Compared with a single project we can expect that the methodology for a programme will emphasize the following aspects of the nine processes.

Table 4.1   Processes within a programme

Governance	The complexities of many parts of the organization having an interest in the programme
Business case and benefits	The interaction of the benefits of different projects and the management of an overall business case
Business acceptance of change	The coordinated management of widespread change towards a future state (a future state that will affect very many stakeholders) Complexity of messages and target audiences. The programme might be of such scale that external communications becomes important (to industry analysts, rating agencies or customers)
Project initiation, planning and staging	The use of project stages is developed into formal cycles of the programme. The mind set is that external change is accepted, not rejected as it is within a project
Project monitoring and control	Programme level control is likely to be focused upon the overall business case, with high-level tracking of milestones from subordinate projects, dependencies and programme risks
Financial management	The need to balance a coherent business case for the overall programme with local interests and budgets. The need to adjust budgets as the goals and capacity of the organization change
Quality management	Focused primarily on the aspects that are owned by the programme — the business case and change management. Projects manage their own quality of deliverables, benefits and change
People management	The complexity of managing multiple projects and the skills required to manage change that has a significant impact on wide areas of the organization
Procurement	The opportunities for coordinated management of suppliers across a number of projects. The scale of the programme might also allow more innovative approaches including outsourcing and supplier partnerships

I propose, therefore, that the core processes are the same as for projects; the differences are about complexity, the broader organizational impact of a programme and a programme's unique, iterative life cycle. The usual descriptions of programme management unfortunately emphasize the differences between project and programme management rather than the common factors.

I recognize the danger of oversimplifying this discussion; from the previous descriptions we can see that a programme has much greater complexity and business impact than a project. Hence it will be more subject to political influences and the role of the programme team and their level of skills will be different to that of a project. But remembering that we are trying to achieve the same purpose as a project should guide us to avoid making programmes feel too special or different, particularly in a BAU organization where these approaches and disciplines are always subject to accusations of complexity and bureaucracy.

I would, though, like to touch on the importance of the benefits and change management processes and the organization structure of programmes, as these have particular relevance in managing programmes in BAU organizations.

In Chapter 3 we showed how the management of business benefits and change were important elements of the approach to managing a business change project. From the definitions of programme management given above, though, it is plain that these processes are at the heart of programme management.

Other processes might become more complex, but these two processes become the very core of what the programme is trying to achieve. Individual projects will of course generate business benefits and business change from the deliverables that they create, but the programme does not make deliverables. Its central goal is to manage the benefits and business change created by the various projects.

So the processes for managing benefits and change deserve particular mention when discussing programme management.

MANAGING BENEFITS

Benefits provide the key lever through which the programme exerts control. On the journey to some desired future state it is the relative benefits of the projects that influence how the programme framework prioritizes the allocation of resources and investment funds.

We have already mentioned (in Chapter 3 and Appendix 1) how the discipline of benefits management can be applied at the project level. A programme is a much broader, more complex environment and we can imagine that, as a central process for the programme, our approach to benefits management is going to be correspondingly more sophisticated.

The sum of the benefits of the various projects within the programme represents the overall business case for the programme and, if properly arranged, the overall business case should exceed the sum of the various parts because project deliverables can be used to reinforce one another. For example, a programme to deliver improved customer service in a bank might include a new call centre. In addition to providing its direct benefits of cost efficiencies in staffing and reduced telecommunications charges, the call centre will contribute to the bank's ability to cross-sell additional products to customers. If the programme also includes a project to implement customer relationship management processes and software, then they also will have cross-selling benefits. Planned with care, can we make the aggregate benefits of cross-selling more than the sum of the parts?

It is the assertion of benefits management that we can indeed make the overall business case more than the sum of its parts, by maximizing benefits as well as coordinating the efforts of multiple projects to optimize the costs and resources required.

I hope the reader can see from these techniques that we are not using benefits management simply as a means to collate the aggregate benefits of the programme – when it would merely be keeping score. We are using benefits management as the core process to select the projects that form the programme, to maximize the benefits case and to prioritize how the projects and benefits are delivered.

Programmes, because they are divided into cycles of change, force a discipline of shorter delivery times and more tangible benefits from each cycle. On many large-scale projects the early stages produce deliverables that are enablers of future work but do not in themselves directly produce benefits. Managed in isolation, it would be quite usual for the first stage of our call centre project to be a feasibility study or location study; both are valuable steps in the project but if the business environment changes and we decide to stop the project then these deliverables produce no lasting benefit to the organization. Managed within a programme, the focus upon lasting benefits from each cycle would prompt a discussion about other potential benefits. For example, the project team might be encouraged to also include some simple process improvements in the current call centre, which will still be of lasting benefit if we do not proceed with the entire project.

One common difficulty is to decide which benefits require the programme management framework to be in place and which (often recurring) benefits can be delivered through the BAU organization.

A programme will typically produce a range of direct benefits in the short term (an acquisition integration programme could achieve benefits perhaps related to cost efficiencies from the use of common technology platforms). There will also be some longer-term benefits (perhaps there will be opportunities in time to cross-sell products to the enlarged customer base or opportunities to manage risk and capital better). These longer-term benefits might also be within the goals of the programme or it might be felt that the programme has done its work when the initial integration activity has been completed and the longer-term benefits are a BAU responsibility to achieve. This is a case for judgement.

MANAGING CHANGE

While the changes created by an individual project are often quite limited in their impact, we can imagine that the cumulative effects of a programme are going to create significant change in the organization. Every organization is unique, of course, but a typical financial services organization might have between five and ten strategic goals, each of which might require a change programme. Each programme will have a significant impact upon the organization.

Programme management helps to manage the challenge of this significant change in two ways:

- The programme's alignment with a strategic goal allows it to articulate a future state that the collective efforts of the various projects will achieve. This could be a specific strategic goal, but is often depicted as a blueprint of how the organization will look when the programme has concluded its work. This description of a future state helps the programme to react as market situations change, adjusting the priorities and mix of projects to achieve the goal.

- The programme manages activity in a series of cycles. The nature of the programme life cycle is that, as each cycle concludes, there will be a period of re-appraisal as the programme plans the shape of the next cycle. This pause coincides with the delivery of the change that the previous cycle had generated and also provides an opportunity for many stakeholders in the organization to adapt to the changed operating practices that have been delivered. These pauses are often referred to as islands of stability.

This staged approach to change allows the programme to set relatively short-term goals for staff, which helps motivation as staff can see tangible benefits. For most programmes, individual projects should have deliverables in 3–9 month periods and the overall programme should have cycles of 6–12 months.

The staged way in which the programme proceeds is not dissimilar to the way in which complex projects can proceed. In Chapter 3 we discussed the staged approach that is often used in financial services and other BAU organizations to implement projects such as new software applications – where the work is staged by country or functionality and this allows the project team to learn from their experiences and improve later parts of the roll-out. As I will repeat later in this book, the boundaries between projects, programmes and (later) portfolios are not sharp and often the difference is one of emphasis rather than of the principles being applied.

Given the scale of the change that a programme creates, it is often the case that its stakeholders include external parties as well as internal parties. These might be industry analysts who are interested in the strategic development of the organization, government regulators, customers or alliance partners. This has implications for how the programme is organized and the seniority of resources and skills that it requires.

ORGANIZATION DESIGN

In Chapter 3 we discussed the organizational model for a project and the key roles of strategic sponsor, accountable executive and project manager. These three roles complement one another with their respective responsibilities for strategic alignment, business needs and solution delivery.

We can build the organizational model for a programme upon this foundation. We will still have a single strategic sponsor and an accountable executive for the programme. The key difference is that the programme, which will have a broad impact upon the organization, will in addition have a number of accountable executives for the subordinate projects. For example, a programme to integrate the acquisition of another bank would include the following accountable executives:

- business line managers, responsible for integrating the new products and customers into the acquiring bank's business and strategies;

- legal functions, responsible for transferring and revising various contractual agreements;

- operations managers, responsible for generating operating efficiencies from the acquisition;

- corporate affairs, responsible for showing external stakeholders that the acquisition is generating the desired benefits and protecting customers' interests;

- technology managers, responsible for integrating various systems without causing a loss of service to customers;

- human resources, responsible for managing staff satisfaction through a period of uncertainty and change.

Each of these accountable executives has their own reporting lines into their BAU structure, but the accountable executive for the integration programme has an overall goal to which they each contribute. The role of the programme manager is to provide the management framework through which the projects can deliver the desired business goals.

The role of the programme manager is therefore very different to that of a project manager. The project manager is focused upon the deliverables of a complex task. The programme manager is much more focused upon managing the business case of the programme, prioritizing projects and on shepherding a range of projects towards their objectives. In each of these activities the programme manager must recognize that responsibility is shared with others, who will have different and competing objectives on other projects and BAU activity.

The programme manager has to manage in an atmosphere of uncertainty, ambiguity and a changing external environment.

This role of programme manager includes:

- managing the business case and the evolving scope of work of the programme (including maintaining the blueprint of a future state and setting the cycles that will be used to progress towards that future state);

- managing communications to multiple stakeholders;

- planning and controlling the change management process;

- oversight of the various projects (milestones, risks and issues rather than detailed control, which is left to project managers).

This is a demanding set of responsibilities and the typical programme will have a team to help the programme manager undertake these responsibilities. While the needs of each programme and the available skills might demand some variations in structure or some aggregation of tasks, the programme manager typically needs the following support on a programme of any size and complexity:

- someone to maintain the blueprint – a business architect;

- someone to manage change and communications – a change manager;

- a programme management office to monitor progress, costs, risks, issues, quality assurance and documentation;

- someone to manage the benefits case (which can sometimes be included in the role of either the change manager or PMO);

- (usually) someone to coordinate the efforts of technology across the various subordinate projects.

See Figure 4.6.

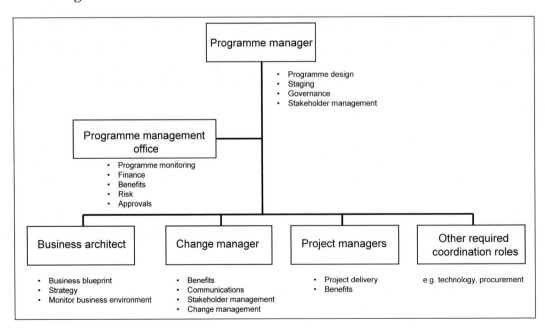

Figure 4.6   **The role of the programme manager**

3 SUCCESSES OF PROGRAMME MANAGEMENT

FOCUS ON BENEFITS

Programmes are management frameworks for delivering benefits. So it should come as no surprise that by implementing programme management an organization should improve its attention to the benefits of projects. While each project should have a benefits case, many projects do not pay sufficient attention to this and become focused entirely upon the deliverables of the project rather than its business benefits. This is particularly prevalent when a project has a significant technology element and when this is not counterbalanced by a strong sponsorship from business line management. Both of these conditions are frequently met in BAU organizations.

For proof of this, look for the projects in your organization that have been given names related to the narrow solution deliverables rather than the broader business goal. Do you have an 'intranet roll-out' project or an 'improved internal communications' project? Do you have a 'new general ledger applications' project or a 'finance re-engineering' project?

The focus upon benefits that a programme brings (and the more senior audience who now govern its progress) makes project teams much more conscious of the delivery of the contribution that is being made to a strategic goal that is recognized across the organization. Teams are more likely to question how project deliverables lead to business outcomes and business benefits. The role of the programme management team increases the focus as they use the various benefits cases to prioritize projects. The concept of benefits enters our executive glossary.

This is not an overnight change and very few BAU organizations could claim to have fully implemented benefits management. Could your organization claim that the benefits of a proposed project are clearly quantified, tracked during the life of the project and then tracked into BAU to ensure that someone is responsible for the delivery of benefits after the project is over? Could an accountable executive show how those benefits have been added into BAU performance targets?

AN INTEGRATED APPROACH TO MANAGING CHANGE

Programmes, as management frameworks to align projects with strategic goals, have also proved their worth in improving how business change is conducted. Year 2000 programmes demonstrate this well. In most banks, Year 2000 was recognized as a business-critical challenge. With a deadline that could not be moved it was realized that activities across the organization had to be marshalled such that the risk of serious failures was removed. The use of programme management structures provided a coordinated approach to the challenge across an organization so that the best use was made of common resources in technology and business functions and so that the allocation of resources was made based upon the centralized management of risk (the prime benefit in this programme being a reduction in risk).

Leaving aside the question of whether there was an exaggerated assessment of the risk on Year 2000, it is undeniable that the use of organization-wide programmes helped manage the challenge so that the level of risk was significantly reduced and that this was done in a coordinated way across the organization.

MULTI-PROJECT ISSUES

While I mentioned earlier that programme management is much more than the management of multiple projects, a programme approach certainly does allow better management of various aspects of running multiple projects. It allows the organization to take an aggregate view of resources across a number of projects. It also allows dependencies between projects to be managed. Programme management also provides some oversight that the various projects are being conducted in a consistent manner and that consistent solutions are being leveraged. This could include that technology investments are made on consistent platforms and enabling technologies, so programmes can optimize not just the benefits to the organization but the cost of making the various deliverables.

TRANSITION TO BAU

This focus upon a more integrated way of managing change and controlling multiple projects also helps BAU organizations to better manage the transition of project activity into BAU operations. The various changes are more easily placed in the bigger picture of organizational change, the impact upon staff can be aggregated and activities to change attitudes, skills or practices can be better coordinated.

GOVERNANCE

Finally, and this is important for the reasons outlined in Chapter 3, programmes allow more efficient governance of projects. The steering processes and committees are inevitably focused more on policy matters and key decisions (because of the breadth of activity of the programme) so are guided to take the right sort of strategic decisions rather than diving into the detail of the conduct of each project. In addition, their governance role can be conducted more efficiently than if they try to govern multiple projects on an individual basis.

As we have discussed before, the effective management of change and the complexities of project governance are two of the most significant areas for project failure. The failure to deliver planned business benefits is widespread. So the way in which programme management addresses these issues can deliver significant achievements to the organization.

4 PROBLEMS IN APPLYING PROGRAMME MANAGEMENT

However, there are also some serious issues with the deployment of programme management in BAU cultures. Some of these are inherent in either the approach or in the culture of BAU organizations and therefore require us to consider carefully how the approach is proposed and deployed.

I suggest that others are a result of how the project management profession has developed the methodology of programme management, in a way that has made it much harder to accept in BAU organizations.

The issues come in the areas of benefits management, the ability of programmes to act as agents of change, bureaucracy and the notion that a company's complete strategic agenda can be described as a set of programmes.

BENEFITS MANAGEMENT

First of all, there is an issue that hits at the very heart of programme management. It is a very uncomfortable fact to those who try to promote programme management, but no one in the business likes the concept of benefits management!

Benefits management is at the heart of programme management, but whereas people do not object to the principles of change management they typically resist (and strongly) the techniques of benefits management. It is a very difficult approach to embed and it is not hard to see why. It promotes a transparency of project returns that sounds great in theory but is resisted strongly in the real world. In the real world, we each like some room for manoeuvre, so we do not want perfect transparency of our actions. We would far rather bundle together the various objectives that we have been set by our manager, so if our current project fails to deliver its business benefits we can perhaps cross-subsidize it from cost or revenue benefits from elsewhere in BAU. Alternatively we can bundle BAU and projects together and blame any underperformance on macroeconomic factors ('GDP did not grow in our markets as planned') or competitive pressures ('the competition has driven prices down to a level that we cannot match').

This might sound cynical, but it is what happens in the real world and in many BAU companies, particularly where senior staff are strongly motivated by bonus payments.

It is particularly difficult to promote the open management of benefits when the programme cuts across a number of business divisions (quite common) and each division might be reluctant to discuss the detail of its business case openly with other divisions or head office.

Second, line managers in the business often change their roles before the programme runs its course and the ownership of new managers taking over existing programmes is usually weaker than that of the programme originators, so programmes weaken and fade away, as do their benefits cases. This is very different to what happens in projectized organizations, where the objectives of the project or programme are less subject to interpretation and where the external need for the programme mitigates against changes of objectives. In a projectized organization, the role of the new programme manager is focused simply on successful completion of the project, not on the ongoing management of a BAU function of which the project is merely a part.

Third, it is very difficult to differentiate between programme benefits and BAU benefits on most projects – even with benefits management techniques. Did the growth in a retail banking division's revenues come from:

- the new branch that was launched recently (easy to measure);

- the new products that have been launched (easy to measure);

- the cross-selling of more products to the average customer as a result of a project to better manage customer relationship information (difficult but possible to assess);

- staff changes or incentivization unrelated to new projects;

- a general increase in business activity in the area, not any particular project?

If it is difficult to segregate the benefits from BAU business growth, who is going to put in the effort to do this? Where a single project has been delivered in a BAU organization it is unlikely to be the project team, for they have been re-assigned to another project or a line role. The tracking will only happen if the accountable executive sees this as personally beneficial, and often this is not the case. The situation is better with a programme team in place, as they remain in place after each stage of the programme, but they are still directed by the accountable executive so they might not have true independence.

So, in the real world, I suggest that benefits management, the central process in the programme, is actually very difficult to fully embed in the organization. It has to be mandated by someone at the top of the organization and someone has to be tasked with ensuring that it happens, or it will not succeed.

Finally, in this discussion of benefits management, comes a failure of the project management profession. The more purist of us, when we took with enthusiasm to programme management, have sold a vision of programmes that downgrades projects.

'Projects just make deliverables; it is the programme that delivers benefits.'

This simplistic view has done great harm to how projects are perceived, but it is also patently untrue. Certainly some projects will generate benefits that are not directly measurable, because they are enablers for other activity. These projects can be justified more easily if they are contained within a programme and their contribution to the broader goal is recognized. The implementation of some new hardware or operating software is difficult to justify on its own, but has value as a part of a programme, where it will provide the platform for new business applications that have specific, tangible benefits.

However, it is unrealistic to take this argument to extremes and argue that individual projects do not have their own benefits without the surrounding framework of a programme. As described earlier, a programme to improve customer service might include a call centre project, for example, which will have its own direct benefits in cost efficiencies for staff and reduced telecommunications charges as well as the potential benefits from cross-selling additional products.

This over-simplified (and plain wrong!) view of the world has had a negative impact for it has:

- damaged attempts to manage benefits at the project level;

- diluted the organization's focus on benefits;

- constrained project managers within a simple delivery role rather than a broader stewardship of the business case.

AGENTS OF CHANGE?

There are other issues with programmes in BAU organizations. We members of the programme management profession tend to have a very purist view of a programme and its management team. We think that, as they are designed as agents of change, they will reinvent themselves as the business needs evolve and as the outside world changes. So they will grow larger and smaller and change their composition as the business needs dictate. Eventually, when their role has been achieved they will decide to disband themselves.

I am not convinced that they really do act in this way in most organizations. Perhaps the career programme manager is happy to move from one programme to another with limited job security, but most programme staff, drawn as they are from BAU functions, desire some more stability.

Whereas projects can be finished quite quickly (in just a year or so), longer-term programmes tend to acquire a life of their own. They have annual budgets that are fought for each year; they defend themselves against the rest of the organization; they seek to preserve their role rather than continually questioning it and reinventing themselves. In short, they start to act like departments, not change agents.

A wise sage once told me, 'When a project or programme team start to place potted plants in their work area, start worrying that they have lost sight of their original objectives of creating change.' Check it out in your organization!

BUREAUCRACY

If the above challenges are inherent in the BAU culture, our profession has also not helped in how it has defined programme management.

Much of the writing about programme management has a heavy emphasis on the programme organization. By comparison, the descriptions of the techniques of managing benefits and change are often brief. As I have mentioned above, this emphasis on structure is quite understandable if we agree that the core processes of programme management are the same as project management and the differences are more about complexity and the iterative programme life cycle. However, the way in which we typically describe programme management has not helped because it makes programme management feel increasingly like a bureaucratic overhead, feeding negative perceptions in a BAU organization that already has a tendency to think of project management as an overhead rather than a necessary condition of successful project delivery.

This bureaucracy is not just a matter of perception. With this emphasis on structure, programmes have indeed produced bureaucracies in many companies:

- heavy programme structures that the business does not feel add value;
- programme offices generating bottom-up data that seems to add limited value when the business is struggling to address top-down problems including continually reacting to changes in the marketplace.

With a heavy infrastructure of expensive people, it becomes harder for the programme to make benefits that are greater than the sum of the parts, so the very rationale for the programme is questioned.

THE COMPANY-WIDE PROGRAMME OF CHANGE

Related to the false assumption that individual projects cannot create business benefits is the assumption that all projects have to reside within a programme and that the strategic agenda of the organization could therefore be defined, comprehensively, by a set of 10 or 12 change programmes. Again, this is a simplistic view of the business world and of the change agenda for the typical organization. There are two issues with this vision.

First, some projects do not fit naturally within a broader programme of change and the strategic agenda is likely to be progressed through a number of programmes supplemented by a number of individual projects. These individual projects might be research projects that are not yet a part of a defined business programme, or opportunistic ventures or infrastructure projects that provide capabilities to all of the programmes; for example communications infrastructure.

Second, this view that the change agenda of the organization can be neatly and fully fitted in a collection of programmes just does not match the real world. Read any case study of a chief executive's campaign to significantly improve an organization's performance and different types of change activity can be identified (on the lines of the hard and soft projects that we discussed in Chapter 2). The harder projects lend themselves to a 'programmatic' approach, as we deliver new processes, organizational structures, products or other capabilities.

The softer projects are focused upon cultural changes within the organization. In this category we will find the initiatives to improve aspects of the organization's culture, communicate a clearer view of the organization's strategies and goals, improve employee engagement, encourage leadership development and promote a distinct, differentiated set of corporate values and behaviours. I intentionally refer to these as 'initiatives' because to varying degrees they do not rely upon a rigorous project management approach. They will still require a structured approach, of course, but the critical success factors will be different, such as the personal actions of and examples set by the senior management. Such actions are often deeply symbolic and touch on the core values and behaviours that are deemed critical to the organization – such as the chief executive of a bank who spends time in branches to reinforce the importance of customer service.

Both types of change activity are critical to achieving a significant transformation in the organization's performance. However, any chief executive will be spending more time and emotional energy on the second type than on the first, as the second type creates the environment within which the first can succeed.

If we continue to promote a simplistic view of the company-wide agenda for change being simply a collection of programmes, then we will continue to harm the concept of programme management and continue to struggle to engage senior executives because our solution does not appear to match their most pressing priorities.

5 MAKING IT HAPPEN

BENEFITS MANAGEMENT

Benefits and change management are the key processes that acquire increased importance when implementing programme management. Earlier we have discussed that benefits management is difficult to embed in the organization and this leaves us with a quandary, because it is also the core message that we must get across to managers within the organization. If we can get managers to accept that benefits management is the core process that we are trying to implement, then we can avoid some of the pitfalls of programme management, in particular the danger of programme management being seen just as an organizational issue and a management overhead.

In many BAU organizations I recommend that we do not try to publicize programme management at all. We should focus almost entirely on implementing benefits management. When explaining benefits it can gradually become apparent to stakeholders that, if we collect together the projects that have common goals as well as common resources, then we will have a greater chance of delivering benefits. Collecting together the projects will require some form of management framework and central coordination.

In other words, we do not promote programme management at all, but we sell the concept of benefits management.

Therefore, it is critical that we find a way to overcome the reluctance of BAU organizations to introduce benefits management. This has to come from the top of the organization, through some form of mandate that change projects will have a clear benefits case and that this case will be monitored through into BAU operations.

In addition to a top-down mandate, a number of reinforcement measures will have to be used to successfully embed programme management in the organization. Such measures will be unique to each organization, but we can assemble a list of typical measures, some of which we have already discussed in Chapter 4:

- Each project must have a clear benefits case to gain approval. If we first introduce the use of benefits management on individual projects and then wait until the organization starts to observe that the benefits cases of various projects have overlaps and dependencies, then we can respond with a proposal to manage various related projects in a more coordinated, programmatic way so that the benefits cases are maximized.

- There must be a way to track business benefits after project completion. As mentioned above, this is no simple task. If we have formed corporate PMOs then they can track business benefits for all programmes and projects. Their independence and ongoing role can allow the organization to monitor the benefits after go-live of the programme (and any ongoing costs such as amortization and support that must be set off against the stream of benefits).

- Some time after each project goes into live use there should be a business benefits review. BAU organizations use a variety of formal review mechanisms to assess business performance and risk. In banks, for example, there is a strong audit culture, with audit focused upon managing risks, poor practice in business controls and the efficient use of the organization's resources. Audit reports are treated as significant events and there is generally a culture of rigorously documenting how management addresses each finding. It would be natural if audit's review of key programmes included a business benefits review and the assessment that a business investment had achieved its claimed benefits. For BAU organizations in other sectors, there will be a similar, formal process that could be used as a host to assess business benefits.

- Benefits of approved projects should be added into the personal/annual performance objectives of the accountable executive.

ORGANIZATION AND CULTURE

We should use the principles outlined earlier to arrive at an organizational model that appears simple. Give as much emphasis to the various projects within the programme as is given to the control function at the centre of the programme. Further promote this focus on the whole programme, not just its centre, by carefully assessing the workload of the central programme team and consolidating roles where possible. On all but the largest of programmes, this is possible and reduces the accusation of programme management becoming an overhead.

The programme management team must complement this simple organizational model with the appropriate culture on the programme. It is a critical mistake, made by many newly appointed programme directors, to portray the programme as a hierarchy. When many of the stakeholders have a loose association with the programme and have other stakeholders of their own, this approach leads to political turf problems. The programme must be portrayed more softly, as a means to coordinate related activities, as a means for related areas to collaborate for the common good, as a vehicle for shared governance of related investments across the organization, but a vehicle that recognizes local ownership and governance of each contributing project.

In the UK, a key reference work for the management of programmes is the publication *Managing Successful Programmes* (MSP). This valuable publication covers the concepts of programme management, the organization of programmes and programme management processes. When discussing programme organizations it refers to the key roles of sponsor (termed the 'senior responsible owner'), a programme manager (responsible for delivering new capabilities to the organization) and a business change manager (who is focused on benefits definition and the transition of programme activity into BAU). It is noted that there could be multiple change managers where a programme affects multiple parts of the organization.

The guide notes the importance of the business authority or architect as a subset of the programme manager role and the provision of a programme management office to support the programme manager with administration, discipline and monitoring.

I believe that this work has played a valuable role in collating best practice on programme management. Consistent with a theme of this book, though, I suggest there are still some areas where a change in emphasis would make the MSP model even more relevant to BAU organizations. These are to match the model that I have described earlier and Table 4.2 describes both the structural changes and changes in emphasis.

The MSP model clearly recognizes the concept of multiple project teams and multiple change managers. My approach builds on this concept, but emphasizes the importance of this distributed business ownership of the benefits case by using accountable executives in each affected business area. Strengthening the business ownership of the subsidiary parts of the programme significantly affects the culture of the programme. It will be more collaborative in nature than the MSP model (which focuses on the hierarchy and central direction of the programme) and I believe that this is more in tune with the realities of delivering change across varied parts of an organization.

I recognize, though, that the central direction of the programme must have the capability to show leadership, or it will be relegated to a support service for project planning which will provide inadequate direction to the effort. In order to demonstrate this leadership the central team must contain some business change skills and business knowledge, through the change manager and business architect.

ROLES AND SKILLS

Having been quite prescriptive above about the various roles that are needed on a programme, this should now be qualified. There can be some ambiguity between the roles of programme manager and accountable executive on programmes in the real world. In some cases, it is quite logical that they are combined. For example, in the earlier example of integrating an acquisition, the future line manager of the integrated business is the logical choice to cover both roles – a combination of accountable executive (who owns the benefits that will accrue to the business after integration) and programme manager (who drives the various workstreams in the programme, probably through a team that overlaps with the BAU management team).

Table 4.2   **Observations on *Managing Successful Programmes***

Issue	Implications
MSP has just one key business role, that of the senior responsible owner who is closest to my definition of 'accountable executive'	The use of a separate sponsor better reflects the structure of a typical BAU organization. It also provides oversight so that commitment is maintained when accountable executives change and so that a considered decision is made regarding when the programme should make the transition into BAU
Difficulty in finding a hybrid programme manager who has both delivery skills and business expertise	In the MSP approach, this will in practice either result in a programme manager with poor project skills (endangering the progress of the programme) or one with low business expertise (relegating the role of the programme manager to 'planning and controls manager'). Depending upon the nature of the programme and the available individuals, we could: • split the role into a programme director and programme manager; • rely upon the role of the accountable executive as business champion
MSP has the programme manager role as a peer to the business change manager	The business change manager typically resides within a BAU role. There will be multiple such managers on a complex programme. There is an assumption that the coordination of project activity and the coordination of change are merely related, whereas they are in reality part of the same role. This assumption would fragment the programme and dilute the programme manager role. The programme manager should have business change support within the core programme team, so I suggest that the business change manager should report to the programme manager
The challenges of communications and change management in BAU organizations do not receive much attention in the MSP, which describes communications briefly (feeling like a responsibility to provide updates) and describes change quite scientifically in terms of benefits, new business architectures and process change	More emphasis should be placed in the programme team on designing the team to manage communications and change. Retain the communications strategy within the programme manager's overall role, but delegate the detailed action plan to the business change manager, where it is an essential complement to managing change and benefits
Recognizing that subsidiary projects have other owners and stakeholders MSP recognizes this, but tends to show multiple business change managers as the owners of change	I prefer the term of 'multiple accountable executives' to ensure the senior governance that is so critical to business change in BAU organizations. This is stronger than the MSP definition of business change managers
Criticality of business architects	The role is described as a part of the programme manager role; for many change programmes, this does not recognize the criticality of the role and a dedicated person with appropriate business skills should be provided

In other cases, there is logic in separating the two roles. A complex programme to introduce customer relationship management processes and technologies might have an accountable executive who is the business manager responsible for distribution channels or customer service; with many other goals on that person's agenda, it is likely that a full-time programme manager will still be required to champion the programme across the organization and make sure that the business case and benefits are developed as business needs dictate.

The term 'programme director' can be used for the most strategic programmes and/ or to reflect the sharing of the two key programme roles, as in the acquisition example above. A strategic programme such as the Basel II programme featured in Chapter 3, where the local ownership and governance of the programme is strong, might only need a programme director supported by a programme office team and some technical specialists at the centre, whereas a programme requiring much more centralized control of the various projects might also require a programme manager below the programme director to handle this enhanced control function.

The main point here is to be pragmatic and apply a model that follows the principles of programme management without becoming a slave to fixed definitions and roles; then the model will feel more natural to the organization and less of a management overhead. Identifying a set of roles that matches available skills as well as the needs of the programme is also essential. This takes us back to an earlier discussion: the vision of a hybrid programme manager with all of the skills, attributes and characteristics required to guide a complex programme as well as the relevant business expertise is an optimistic one. Following a model of programme management as an embedded skill, we are likely to best fill the role with a combination of business leadership, project management and change management skills.

GOVERNANCE

Programmes, like projects, need an appropriate governance structure to engage stakeholders and ensure that progress is achieved and that the goals of the programme remain valid for the organization.

The governance structure for a programme will be complex and will evolve during the life cycle. Consistent with its staged nature, the programme will also have to submit itself for approval at a number of points during its life cycle.

In addition to this direct governance, programmes need some additional oversight to ensure that they remain in line with strategy and that they disband at the right time. This is best provided in the context of the organization's complete agenda for change and will be addressed in Chapter 5.

Finally, there should be personal or team-based incentives to ensure that the programme does indeed disband at the right time and does not drift into justifying its ongoing existence. This is a key issue for the strategic sponsor to consider and address.

TOOLS

This discussion builds upon the description of tools in Chapter 3, where we focused upon collaboration across multiple stakeholders rather than the traditional, logistical control approach from the world of hard projects.

Let's now review the picture of a change programme that has been painted in this chapter. It includes the following characteristics:

- scope that regularly changes, but is allocated into tranches of activity to provide control and accountability;

- a programme structure designed to deliver strategic change in a concerted manner;

- a broad community of stakeholders, including project teams and accountable executives whose allegiance is not solely to the programme;

- a focus at the programme level on business change, benefits and monitoring the external environment for changes that will affect the course of the programme;

- a focus at the project level on project delivery (deliverables, costs, resources, quality, risk and project benefits);

- common interests across the programme; either resources, dependencies or the aggregate benefits case.

As we discussed in Chapter 3, we have a disparate community of stakeholders, many of whom do not fit the traditional picture of a team member or project manager. They want information that is filtered and prioritized according to their needs and provided at a level of detail that suits them.

Programmes are inevitably more complex and cross-functional than projects, so it is even more important that the tools that we use should facilitate the transfer of information across the programme.

With our focus at the programme level being on business change, benefits and monitoring the external environment for changes that will affect the course of the programme, simple project management tools are not going to be appropriate for managing a programme. Such tools will provide resource and task information and will aggregate it to give a multi-project overview but their use for managing a programme is limited by this focus on tasks and resources.

Programme management tools are aimed at addressing the integrated nature of the programme. Early entrants into this field were still driven by project management methodologies and were primarily aggregators of multi-project information, focused on the management of costs and resources, and occasionally benefits. This aggregation of information leads to a very hierarchical view of the programme, which is:

- contrary to the collaborative, cross-functional approach that change programmes require in complex organizations;

- unlikely to help users connect related topics across the programme;

- slow to react to changes in strategy and programme scope.

Aggregation of project information does not inevitably lead to the projects being linked to business goals in a meaningful way.

Hence, the suggestions made in Chapter 3 about considering carefully the right balance of control, collaboration and knowledge management when selecting tools are even more relevant at the programme level.

6 CONCLUSIONS

Programme management has attracted industry debate through the 1990s. Its focus on benefits management and governance has helped to promote the contribution that projects make to the strategic change agenda of companies. It represented the next stage in the maturity of the discipline of project management (recall Figure 2.1).

Programme management has had mixed success in BAU organizations. Some of the reasons for this lie in the cultures of BAU organizations, but I believe that the project management profession has not always helped. In particular, we have made too much of the differences between project and programme management when we are in reality following the same processes, enhanced to reflect the broader impact and complexity of a programme of related projects.

There are some differences, but we should emphasize the common features rather than the differences. If we also focus BAU organizations on the practice of benefits management and simple organizational models that do not feel like bureaucracy, then I believe a programmatic approach to managing related projects can be embedded more successfully into BAU organizations.

There are limits to the application of programme management. Not all change is best delivered in a structured, programmatic manner, so programmes are not the whole answer to the organization's change agenda.

The concept of the multi-talented, hybrid programme manager who can champion the business case internally as well as exhibiting exemplary project management and commercial skills is not realistic across the industry (just as the hybrid business/technology chief technology officers of a decade ago have proved elusive to find or create).

If we can achieve this more realistic operating model, based on an evolution of project management disciplines and skills, there are significant benefits at stake in terms of improved project performance. If we can gain 15–20 per cent improvement in project performance through the use of industry-standard project management disciplines (Chapter 3) then we should be able to target similar improvements through 'doing the right projects'.

Is the excellent management of benefits the whole answer to ensuring strategic alignment of all our projects? Does a programmatic approach to managing change fully close the gap between projects and the strategic goals of the organization as depicted in Figure 4.2?

Even when each project or programme serves its business owner and stakeholders to the best of its ability, we are still left with some further questions to fully close this gap:

- Isn't the measure of strategic value and alignment something more than benefits anyway?

- How can we ensure that a series of programmes across the organization represents the right blend of projects – the right balance of risk and reward, the right priorities between competing business initiatives?

In Chapter 5 I will tackle this next stage in the evolution of project management as a discipline deeply tied into the strategic agenda of the organization.

Projects as Agents of Strategic Change – Portfolio Management

ROADMAP FOR CHAPTER 5

This chapter builds upon the principle established in Chapter 4 – that if projects are to be successful agents of business change then their contribution to the organization's strategic agenda must be clear. Programme management has helped to provide this clarity of contribution, but has not been fully successful, so I will recap on some of the shortcomings of programme management in this regard, then describe the practical application of a technique that seeks to manage all of an organization's change projects and programmes as a portfolio.

This approach has much similarity with portfolio approaches to managing a number of financial investments. It is attracting increased attention as a more complete means of portraying projects within a broader, strategic context and hence of better managing the investment in business change. It also aligns projects with the organization's strategic agenda in a way that is more in tune with the cultures and existing business processes of BAU organizations.

1 INTRODUCTION TO PORTFOLIO MANAGEMENT

It is with some trepidation that I use the term 'portfolio', given the debate that the project management profession has had over the past ten years on the difference between projects and programmes. I hope you will see the differences and why a growing number of companies are considering portfolio management of project investments to be one of their mission-critical processes.

Chapter 4 described the use of programmes as management frameworks to align projects with strategic goals and as agents of business change. It covered the advantages of this approach, which start with better management of multi-project issues such as dependencies and resources, then build with the much better focus

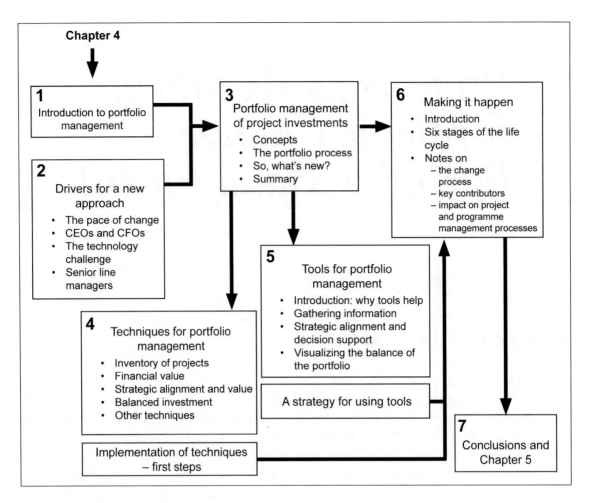

Roadmap for Chapter 5

that programme structures bring to managing change – for example, improved management of the transition of projects into BAU. As change management factors are the key cause of so many project failures, this is a significant benefit.

In addition (and as we would expect because programmes are management frameworks for delivering benefits) we have gained improved attention to the benefits of projects. We question how project deliverables lead to business outcomes and business benefits and we can use this to prioritize projects within a programme. The concept of benefits enters our executive glossary.

However, Chapter 4 also raised some serious issues with the deployment of programme management in BAU cultures. First of all, and it is an uncomfortable fact, no one in the business likes the concept of benefits management. It is a very hard sell. It promotes a transparency of project returns that sounds great in theory but is resisted strongly in the real world, where we each like some room for manoeuvre.

Second, line managers in the business often change their roles before the programme runs its course and the ownership of new managers taking over existing programmes is usually weaker than that of the programme's originators, so programmes weaken, as do their benefits cases. This is very different to what happens in projectized organizations, where the objectives of the project or programme are less subject to interpretation and politics and where changes in the programme manager do not typically result in changes of objectives.

Third, it is very difficult to differentiate between programme benefits and BAU benefits on most projects – even with benefits management techniques.

So, in the real world, I have suggested that benefits management, the central process in the programme, is actually very difficult to fully embed in the organization.

These are significant issues for programme management, but there is a broader concern as well. It seems that controlling benefits, valuable as it is, does not supply the whole answer to ensuring strategic alignment of all our projects. If each project or programme serves its business owner and stakeholders to the best of its ability, with a solid business case, aren't we still left with further questions?

- Isn't the measure of strategic value to the organization something more than benefits anyway? Techniques of benefits management, even when addressing both tangible and intangible benefits, do not seem broad enough to measure strategic value.

- How can we ensure that we have the right blend of projects across the organization – the right balance of risk and reward, of short- and long-term paybacks, of innovation and research projects compared with well-defined business initiatives?

- How can we balance investment across the programmes, and how can we justify investments that cut across all the programmes, for example IT infrastructure? The balance between investing in projects with immediate (customer-facing) business benefits and investing in infrastructure for longer-term benefits is a classical dilemma for BAU organizations and the less attractive infrastructure investments still tend to be left out from the scope of business programmes.

These are real concerns when an organization might be spending 20 per cent of its annual operating budget on projects. Recent industry studies have indicated that about 40 per cent of this investment in business change is wasted due to lack of alignment with business strategy, so perhaps 8 per cent of an organization's operating budget is currently being spent upon initiatives that will not deliver added value.

2 DRIVERS FOR A NEW APPROACH

The concern that programme and benefits management are not the full answer to the problem of aligning change projects with the company's strategic agenda is the key driver for a new approach; and it is felt across the organization.

THE PACE OF CHANGE

BAU organizations are subject to increasing levels of change and volatility in their business. While we all appreciate this fact of business life, we should also reflect that it drives a relentless increase in the proportion of an organization's activity that is dedicated to change (= projects). BAU organizations are typically not structured to address this increasing proportion of change activities (they are, after all, BAU organizations!).

Companies have to face the challenge of too many projects, partly mitigated by the disciplines of programme management, all competing for priorities and all with positive benefits cases. Furthermore, and even with techniques such as staging, the delivery times for the more complex projects and programmes are actually longer than the realistic planning horizon of the company. So, increasingly companies are not merely asking themselves the programme management question of 'Are we doing the right projects?' but are having to regularly ask 'Are we *still* doing the right projects?'. They have been seeking a more holistic means of doing this than programme management.

CEOs AND CFOs

In today's business world, chief executive officers and chief financial officers have many conflicting priorities and concerns when considering investing for the future of their organizations. In a volatile world they need options on the future and the ability to change direction as strategic opportunities and BAU performance change but they are typically faced with a less than perfect process to make investments:

- We have too many projects.

- We never cancel any projects.

- Each project has a positive business case, so why is it that the aggregate impact of the projects is insufficient?

- Our project spend does not match with the key growth areas of the business.

- Where are the benefits?

- This is 20 per cent of our cost base; we do not know what we are getting from it.

THE TECHNOLOGY CHALLENGE

For many BAU organizations, a key component of each change project is technology. The technology function typically has more demand than it can handle. Projects are numerous, so technology costs are rising and as the IT function's budgets make up an increasing share of the company's total budget the pressures have grown upon their leaders – the chief information officers or chief technology officers. Chief executives are asking the hard questions:

- Is technology delivering value from its investments?

- Are the investments aligned with business needs?

- Is technology optimizing its use of resources?

- Are we building the same deliverables many times?

CIOs have been seeking a means of showing the business that they are optimizing investments and responding to ever-changing business needs. They want to do this in a more analytical and structured manner than has been the case historically. However, they typically do not have the right information available because their own management information systems have focused more on the effective use of existing technology assets than on their performance in supporting the business's change agenda.

So, CIOs are looking for a better way of depicting the aggregate contribution that IT makes to the business.

SENIOR LINE MANAGERS

Other managers are also concerned. Project proposals are presented to them in an ad hoc manner, so it is impossible for the managers to prioritize them. Managers also feel that project teams make premature funding requests (to be first past the post in seeking funding) and this means that some later, but valuable projects will not receive funding. Business cases have questionable benefits and the linkage to strategic goals is unclear.

Project proposals are often made after significant analysis by the project team, who therefore want rubber stamp approval, not an open debate about alternative approaches.

In the new millennium, senior managers also face new challenges. The heady days of e-commerce, when business cases were considered as bureaucracy, have been replaced by a new realism and focus on adding shareholder value. Clear accountability for financial control is essential and becoming a personal legal liability with US legislation (Sarbanes-Oxley)[1] likely to be the forerunner of other national legislation.

Senior managers are looking for a more structured process to determine investment priorities than they have traditionally used.

3 PORTFOLIO MANAGEMENT OF PROJECT INVESTMENTS

CONCEPTS

A few companies have been using an approach that manages a set of initiatives in the same way as one might manage a portfolio of financial investments. They are taking an enterprise-wide view of all project investments and are seeking to regularly review that the investments are being made where they return the highest strategic value. The approach typically also includes techniques for assessing that the portfolio is a balanced

---

1   The Sarbanes-Oxley Act of 2002 was passed by the US Congress to protect investors from the possibility of fraudulent accounting activities by corporations.

set of investments – balanced in the sense that its shape matches key strategic goals and is a sensible compromise of risk and reward across the enterprise.

The objective is to arrive at a portfolio of investments that does not necessarily include just the projects that are individually most attractive, but includes the set of projects that collectively best meets the strategic goals of the organization. The approach tries to think in terms of optimization, not merely prioritization.

The companies where this approach has been used are typically in the fast moving consumer goods, chemical and pharmaceutical industries; all industries where a broad range of projects or new products must be managed, where markets can be volatile and where significant bets must be made about future business direction.

Portfolio management uses principles that BAU managers can relate to more easily than the complexities of programme management:

- Just as an investment manager would appraise a portfolio for risk, return and balance and regularly make 'buy, hold, sell' decisions, an organization can appraise and manage a portfolio of projects and start, continue or stop individual projects.

- Just as an investment manager must meet the needs of each customer (including their own desire to assume some risk for a given level of return), an organization must meet various needs from its investment in business change and must satisfy various stakeholders.

- Just as an investment manager wants to make a satisfactory return on investment, an organization wants to be able to effectively allocate its own financial and human resources.

This approach is less prescriptive than the defined disciplines of programme management. It also responds to the other drivers mentioned above. The approach offers a more holistic means to assess projects in the strategic context of the organization.

Recalling the earlier picture (Figure 4.2) of the pyramid where it was suggested that programmes could bridge between business strategies and projects, it seems that portfolio management can provide a more holistic bridging layer between overall business goals and both projects and programmes. See Figure 5.1.

In addition to the concept of a portfolio that is regularly adjusted to suit the organization's strategic goals, these companies have typically also managed projects as a series of stages, each stage ending in a formal review or decision point ('gate') that decides if the project's value still warrants its continued place in the overall portfolio. Just as an investment manager regularly reviews that each investment still warrants a place in the portfolio, the organization wants to know that each project still meets some criteria of worth and should be allowed to continue.

The portfolio management process, therefore, complements a regular review of the worth of the portfolio with a stop/go assessment of each project's unique worth at some regular points in its life cycle. Commentators emphasize that both portfolio review and stage gate processes are required for a successful process, but that the emphasis between the two depends upon the culture and needs of the organization.

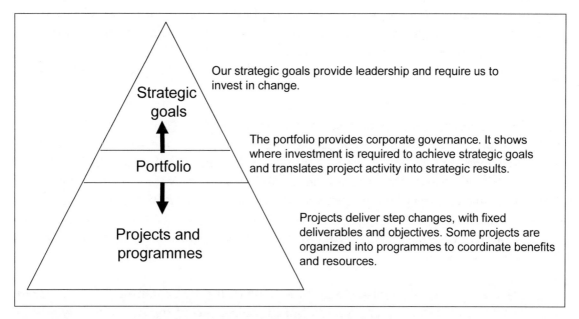

Figure 5.1   Strategic alignment through a portfolio

THE PORTFOLIO PROCESS

In summary, the process is shown in Figure 5.2.

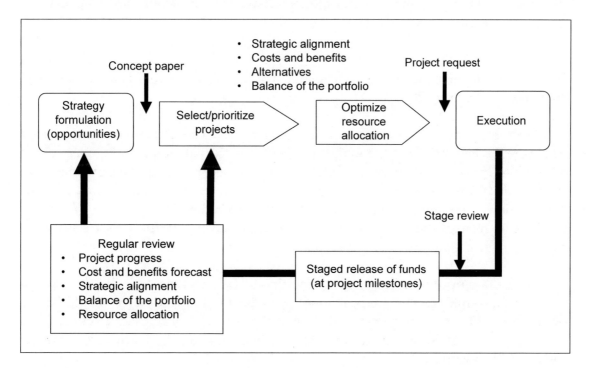

Figure 5.2   The portfolio management process

Potential projects or programmes are put forward for review at as early a stage as possible. A brief statement called a 'Concept Paper' is used to allow management to assess whether the project fits with the financial and strategic goals of the organization. Of course, many BAU organizations will already use some staged form of project approval, but the first management approval often takes place after some initial feasibility work. Under portfolio management we are trying to assess the desirability and strategic fit of a potential project at a much earlier stage. We want the ability to influence events, preventing project teams from closing options that senior management might want investigated.

Based upon strategy, we then select and prioritize projects, not just by benefits but by their strategic value and by their impact upon the performance and balance of the portfolio of existing projects. There are a number of techniques to assist holistic decisions at this stage, using various criteria for the strategic alignment, value and risk of projects. Approval of the concept of the project leads to the project submitting a 'Project Request' for funding; this confirms not just the desirability of the project but its feasibility. On major projects, even this piece of work will require some funding, which the Concept Paper will have sought.

For major projects we also stage the release of funds. Of course this is a feature of project and programme management but in the context of the portfolio it would be pointless to undertake a regular review of the portfolio if one is locked in to a set of long-term projects that prevent any re-balancing of the portfolio. Hence the Project Request will describe both the overall project and, in some greater detail, the costs, deliverables and benefits of the first stage of the project. At the completion of each stage, a 'Stage Review' will seek continued funding. This Stage Review is an updated Project Request, which notes whether previous commitments have been achieved and then makes a request for funding of the next stage.

We continue the portfolio process with regular reviews of the value and balance of the entire portfolio, because in today's volatile world one must regularly ask 'Are we still doing the right projects?'

We need a management forum to review these Concept Papers, Project Requests and Stage Reviews and then to monitor the performance, balance and alignment of the portfolio – a 'project investment committee' (or 'investment board' as some organizations have termed it) that has broad representation from across the organization. In some organizations the committee might be called a 'change coordination committee', reflecting the desire to manage the impact of the changes produced by multiple projects as well as the investment capacity of the organization.

If the organization is made up of multiple divisions, then each division should have such a committee to manage its own portfolio. Group/head office should have a similar committee to manage the aggregate of these portfolios across the organization and to approve cross-business projects, typically for technology infrastructure or merger and acquisition activity.

SO, WHAT'S NEW?

The reader's challenge at this point might be 'Hold on, isn't this just a different way of expressing a programme management approach? It includes a methodology of stages, it focuses on business benefits and it allows the management of multiple and competing projects.'

Of course, the portfolio management approach does share these features, hence is similar in its goals to programme management, but the key differences are that it:

- takes a broad view of the strategic contribution of a portfolio of projects, broader than benefits management, as will become clear later in this chapter when we look at portfolio management techniques;

- adds the concept of balanced investment across the enterprise, allowing us to address concerns such as justifying investment in infrastructure or innovation;

- forces a regular review of investments across the organization (which can be compared with the more localized review that takes place within each programme under a programme management methodology);

- is presented as a top-down view of translating strategy into projects and programmes, which is inherently more in tune with the way that executive BAU management thinks;

- is managed through a business-driven investment committee (that is, as a part of BAU business development) not a discrete or specialist programme steering committee.

SUMMARY

That is the portfolio management process – intentionally simple and focused on provoking top-down debates about strategic alignment as well as bottom-up debates about programme performance. It has been used for some time in companies, but often for product development rather than business change projects.

There are recognized processes and techniques for appraising the value and balance of the portfolio, and increasingly there are tools designed to support the process.

The techniques of portfolio management are worthy of note. The concept of managing investments as a portfolio is quite simple to appreciate. But how, in practice, does one assess the strategic alignment or strategic value of a project? Which factors are important when assessing the balance of the portfolio? It is the answers to these questions that provide the added value of the portfolio management process and show how the theory can be effectively put into practice.

4 TECHNIQUES FOR PORTFOLIO MANAGEMENT

INTRODUCTION

Even though portfolio and programme management share many objectives and features, a key difference is that portfolio management uses various techniques to holistically assess the contribution of the project or programme to the organization's strategic agenda, whereas programme management focuses upon a narrower view of business benefits.

This section describes the techniques available for appraising the portfolio. Because the subject of portfolio management is so critical to the future success of project management disciplines in BAU organizations and because there is such limited literature on the practical application of the techniques, I will describe the standard techniques in more detail than I have done elsewhere in this book.

The techniques, presented in Figure 5.3, are as follows:

- ways to record and display the inventory of projects;
- techniques to appraise the value of the portfolio;
  - purely financial measures of value
  - broader measures of value; strategic alignment and value
- techniques to assess the balance of the portfolio;
- decision support techniques that can be used to optimize a set of projects.

Reliance on a single, traditional measure such as the 'hurdle rate' of a given rate of return provides a very narrow view of the place of a project within the portfolio and cannot recognize the other projects in the portfolio. Ranking systems, another traditional approach to selecting projects, do reflect the other projects in the portfolio but still tend to select a collection of the best individual projects, not the set of projects that collectively

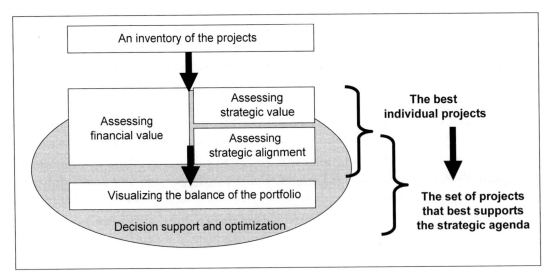

Figure 5.3   The techniques of portfolio management

makes the best contribution to the strategic agenda. Projects for essential technology infrastructure often get excluded through such ranking systems. Interdependencies are not recognized.

Current industry best practice is that a blend of appraisal techniques, including non-financial techniques, results in the best portfolio performance. This improved performance is achieved because a blend of techniques tends to lead us to an optimized portfolio – a group of projects that collectively maximizes the contribution to the strategic agenda of the business.

INVENTORY OF PROJECTS

Spreadsheets are typically used to gather project data from Project Requests and progress reports. The data will include budgets and forecasts for costs and benefits, key milestone dates and the more subjective data that allows us to describe the nature of the project or score the value of the project.

A map of projects illustrates pictorially how each project is associated with a strategic imperative for the organization. See Figure 5.4.

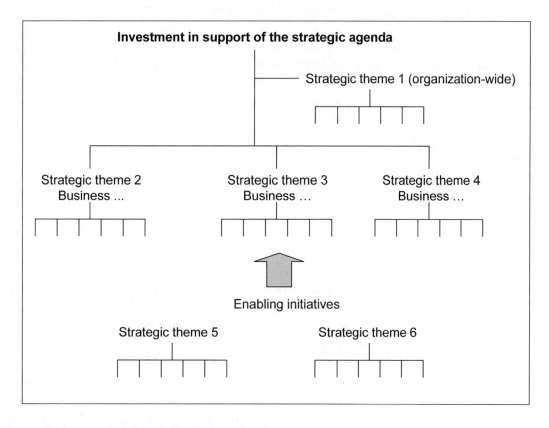

Figure 5.4   Pictoral map of projects

For the project managers amongst us, this technique looks much like the work breakdown structure for a project and it fulfils a similar purpose – showing how the various projects lead to deliverables or business objectives that, in aggregate, amount to the strategic agenda of the organization. This is a key input to the techniques that address strategic alignment and value. It also ranks very highly as a technique to provoke initial management debates about the investment portfolio. See the later section on 'Making it happen'.

FINANCIAL VALUE

Various techniques are available for financial appraisal. They use traditional approaches such as net present value (NPV), complemented by some derived measures that seek to enhance the raw NPV figures:

- net present value

- derivations of NPV (including one which divides NPV by remaining cost to achieve a measure of the leverage that can be achieved from the remaining investment)

- return on investment

- payback period/time to positive cash flow

- expected commercial value (which takes NPV and then factors in the risks of project delivery and subsequent delivery of the benefits).

Despite its limitations (its inherent inaccuracy when calculated in the early stages of a risky project being the major concern) NPV still represents the most popular financial comparison between projects, particularly as the starting point for an organization. Used in isolation, there is a danger that a positive NPV becomes regarded as the sign of a good business case when the return might actually be a poor use of corporate funds. The more holistic view obtained from portfolio management addresses this danger.

But, in today's volatile environment NPV should typically be supported by the use of payback period as a hurdle. The specific hurdle period will be a matter for each organization, but I would propose that, in most markets today, payback periods of longer than two years should only be approved if there is significant strategic value associated with the project and the payback of the overall portfolio remains acceptable.

In time, businesses might wish to improve the use of the NPV measure by dividing NPV by the remaining cost to give a measure of how best to create value from outstanding expenditure (reducing the importance of sunk costs) which will often provide a better portfolio than the use of simple NPV rankings.

Expected commercial value is a refinement of NPV that recognizes the specific risk of each initiative. While this is attractive from an academic viewpoint, for factoring risk into financial appraisal, in many cases the calculation of project risk, particularly that risk related to commercial success, is very prone to error. Hence, initially I would not propose the use of this technique, relying on the simpler assessments of risk that are used in scoring models (see below).

STRATEGIC ALIGNMENT AND VALUE

Allocating investment to strategic themes

The first technique that seeks to assess a broader measure of value uses strategic themes as its basis. It is designed to ensure that money is invested in a way that mirrors the business strategy and strategic priorities. Assembling the portfolio really means setting a spending target for each strategic goal. The way in which money is allocated is inevitably partly subjective, a matter of judgement for the management team, but this simple approach has a number of attractive features:

- It forces a clear alignment of expenditure with strategy through management debate.

- Dissimilar projects do not compete against one another.

- It can be used at both organization and divisional levels.

- Spend between strategic themes can be re-prioritized relatively easily through the year so that total spend remains consistent with the business's targets.

- Projects within a theme can be re-prioritized without affecting the overall portfolio.

We allocate spending targets to each of the strategic themes that have previously been articulated in the map of projects. Figure 5.5 shows what a hierarchy of these themes might look like, at group and divisional levels and reflecting some spend on technology and support infrastructure.

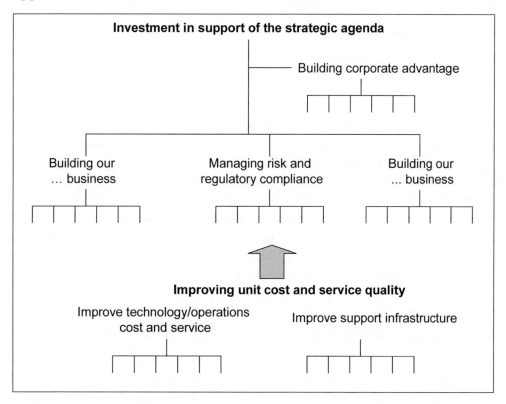

Figure 5.5   Strategic themes

An alternative analysis, which has great appeal when trying to engage executive management teams in debate, looks at the type of benefits produced by the investment. It simply assesses how the investment is allocated between:

- non-discretionary projects (for example, meeting regulatory requirements)
- revenue growth
- revenue protection
- cost reduction
- cost avoidance.

This can be particularly informative in the early stages of the portfolio process.

The strategic themes approach can also be applied to other categories of expenditure, depending on the nature of the organization. For example, how is expenditure allocated between mandatory (regulatory) projects, innovation, infrastructure or business systems/ processes?

In international groups, looking at expenditure by country can prove informative when compared with the target markets that are defined in the business strategy.

There are also a number of industry benchmarks for how expenditure is distributed, an example being the allocation of IT expenditure between:

- infrastructure development
- transactional systems
- informational systems
- strategic advantage.

A variation, which focuses purely on project benefits rather than project expenditure, simply compares, in spreadsheet form, the benefits of all projects in a strategic theme with the overall business growth plans for that area of business. By inspection, one can assess if the contribution of the projects, in concert with organic growth, is reasonable and in line with strategy. If the projects in a given business area produce only a few percentage points of the proposed business growth, then we can challenge if they are worthwhile. If the projects produce a very high percentage of the proposed business growth (or even more than 100 per cent, which can happen!) we can challenge whether the benefits cases claimed by the projects are realistic.

Scoring models

Scoring models are used to overcome the limitations of relying on only a single financial criterion to rank projects (in our case, probably some flavour of NPV). The scoring models typically arrive at an aggregate score for each project that recognizes financial return, strategic importance and an assessment of risk.

Figure 5.6 shows an example of the simpler scoring models. In addition to ranking by NPV, each project is assigned a score for strategic importance and a score for the level of risk associated with the project. The average ranking across the three measures is used as the means of prioritizing the projects.

There are numerous variations on this simple technique. For example, one could calculate an aggregate score for strategic importance and NPV and then multiply this aggregate score by a confidence factor (= risk) to provide a more holistic assessment of strategic value.

The first example integrates scores for NPV, strategic value and risk. Rankings are shown in brackets. The average ranking across the three measures is used for prioritization.

PROJECT	Cost	NPV	Strategic value (1–25)	Risk score (1–15)	Average rank
A	7	16 (1)	15 (1)	13 (4)	2.00 (1)
B	5	12 (2)	10 (3)	10 (2)	2.33 (2=)
C	6	10 (3)	4 (4)	12 (3)	3.33 (4)
D	3	5 (4)	12 (2)	5 (1)	2.33 (2=)

Ranked simply by NPV, we might do projects A, B and C, spending 18 for a potential NPV of 38. On average rankings, we might consider spending only 15 on projects A, B and D (for an NPV of 33) and rejecting C which is risky and of low strategic value.

A variation uses an average score for NPV and strategic value, then multiplies this by a confidence factor. For the same projects A, B, C and D:

PROJECT	Cost	NPV	Strategic value (1–25)	Average	Confidence	Score
A	7	16 = 100%	15 = 60%	80%	70%	56 (1)
B	5	12 = 75%	10 = 40%	57%	80%	46 (2)
C	6	10 = 62%	4 = 16%	39%	75%	30 (4)
D	3	5 = 31%	12 = 48%	39%	95%	37 (3)

Again, the technique provokes a debate about project C based upon its low strategic value. D scores lower than B in this model because the difference in their NPVs is reflected more strongly than in the first ranking model.

Figure 5.6   Scoring models

How does one calculate strategic importance in such a scoring model? Figure 5.7 shows an example of an approach that incorporates several measures to arrive at a measure of strategic value. The specific measures will vary by organization, but the model should include a balanced set of measures, including some that reflect future value (here, positioning is such a measure).

BALANCED INVESTMENT

The methods shown above all seek, in various ways, to maximize the value of the portfolio. First and foremost the portfolio must contain good projects and that is where these maximization techniques are critical.

Criteria	Scoring		Maximum score
Quantifiable benefits generated for...	None	0	
	< 3 years	2	
	> 3 years	4	4
Number of dependent projects	< 5	1	
	6–9	2	
	10+	3	3
Number of countries affected	< 5	1	
	6–9	2	
	10 +	3	3
Business impact	low	1	
	medium	2	
	high	3	
	critical	5	5
Group positioning or participation	assess	0–4	4
Competitive advantage	low	2	
	medium	4	
	high	6	6
			25

Figure 5.7   Assessment of strategic value

But the financial methods consider only financial value and while the other methods take a broader view of value and of strategic alignment, these methods are not sufficient to ensure that the portfolio is well balanced. The list of projects resulting from the use of these techniques could theoretically maximize profits or some other criterion, but might be a very unbalanced portfolio. For example, there might be a poor blend of long-term and short-term projects or a preponderance of high-risk projects.

A further set of techniques is used to look at the portfolio of projects and analyse (usually pictorially as a grid) whether there is an appropriate blend of projects when considering a range of such factors.

There are a number of different grids that can be used to analyse the portfolio. The most obvious, much-used variation is a grid that maps the relative risk and reward of the portfolio of projects. See Figure 5.8 for an example and some observations to which such a technique could lead. Note how some projects, which have positive business cases and so in isolation might look attractive, appear here to be poor investments because their return is small compared to other projects and they have high levels of risk.

A typical set of grid views, for a company starting to use portfolio management, could also include:

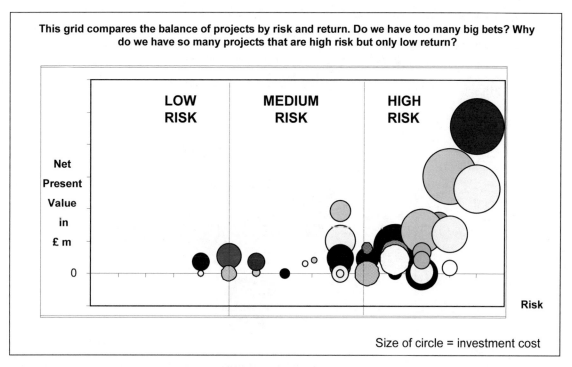

Figure 5.8   Risk vs reward grid

- Short-/long-term trade-offs (see Figure 5.9). Do we have the right balance between short- and long-term projects? Are we happy with the amount we are spending next year on some major investments that will deliver returns much later?

- Internal/external benefits. Is our investment focused upon improving the efficiency or cost of our internal processes, or is it being used to create a better product or service for the customer?

- The business value of IT within projects. Where we are investing in technology, is it being used for operational improvements or are we leveraging technology for business advantage?

This blend of views addresses the key business tensions between risk, reward and time, but also brings in an internal process/customer service viewpoint and brings the use of technology into the debate.

A fuller list of grid views, or 'bubble diagrams' as they are often called, is shown in Table 5.1.

In addition to the grid techniques, other techniques can help to assess the balance of the portfolio. A matrix view of products and countries/markets can be used to show how consistently the organization is implementing products across countries and to highlight opportunities that it is not currently pursuing.

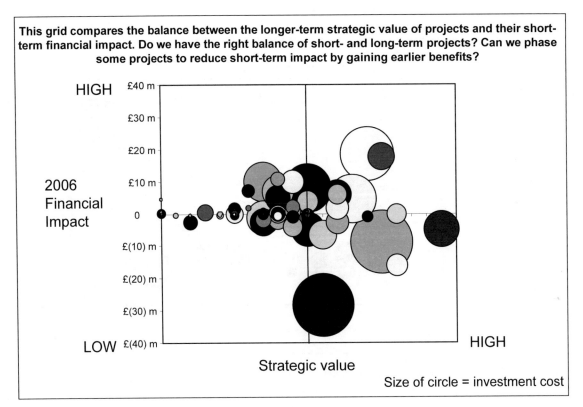

This grid compares the balance between the longer-term strategic value of projects and their short-term financial impact. Do we have the right balance of short- and long-term projects? Can we phase some projects to reduce short-term impact by gaining earlier benefits?

Figure 5.9   Short-/long-term trade-off grid

Table 5.1   Grid techniques for portfolio management

Type of grid	Horizontal axis	Vertical axis
Risk vs reward (Figure 5.8)	Risk rating	Benefits; NPV, gross benefits
Short-/long-term trade-offs (Figure 5.9)	Strategic value	Cost in the next fiscal year
Internal or external benefits (as described above)	Level of customer benefit	Level of process/technology benefit
Business value of IT within projects (as described above)	IT's impact upon operations	IT's impact upon business strategy
Leveraging investment (comparing the scale of investments with return on investment)	Benefits	Cost to implement
Cost vs timing (How much are we spending and what is the speed of return)	Time to implement (e.g. time to first benefits or time to payback point)	Cost to implement
Ease vs attractiveness (desirability of investments)	Ease; a measure of risk and barriers	Attractiveness; a measure of strategic alignment and benefits
Attractiveness vs competitive position (While an investment might appear attractive overall, how does it specifically improve our competitive position?)	Impact upon competitive position	Attractiveness

Technology/operations roadmaps categorize initiatives into new 'platform' developments and 'derivative' projects that leverage or improve existing platforms. This prompts a debate on the right balance between:

- the short-term business benefits that come from derivative projects or tactical solutions (as implementation costs and times are relatively low);

- platform projects that potentially deliver greater benefits but over a longer period and with increased initial investment.

OTHER TECHNIQUES – DECISION SUPPORT

A number of other techniques are available, generally classified as decision support systems. They use mathematical models to help decision making, examples being:

- analytical hierarchy process, which uses forced pair comparisons to make choices between projects;

- optimization techniques, which attempt to find the optimal set of projects that maximizes an objective (for example, profit) subject to a set of resource constraints (for example, cost or people) and inter-dependencies;

- real options techniques, which view the stages within a project as the purchase of a series of options to make future investments.

These techniques often require tool support and specialist process knowledge from external consultants, so they can be costly. They also require high quality data to achieve meaningful results.

IMPLEMENTATION OF TECHNIQUES – FIRST STEPS

Current industry best practice is that a blend of appraisal techniques, including non-financial techniques, results in the best portfolio performance. Using purely financial measures results in poor portfolio performance.

An organization will make best progress if it starts the portfolio management process with a relatively simple set of techniques. As the process matures, the company can evolve the techniques, becoming more sophisticated in the approach and reflecting the specific needs of each business area. In fact, during discussions that I have held with other companies where portfolio management is becoming a well-embedded process, it was actually common, and a salutary warning, that as the organizations have matured they have used fewer portfolio techniques, not more!

From the variety of techniques available, it is proposed that the following, relatively simple, techniques would typically be used initially:

- spreadsheets and the pictorial map of projects to provide the inventory of projects and project data;

- NPV as the measure of financial value, supported by assessing payback period and other key financial measures that are relevant for the company (for example, in banks the cost/income ratio is keenly watched by industry observers and so could be included as a primary measure for the impact of the portfolio upon the overall business);

- allocation of investment by strategic themes (Figure 5.5), supported by comparisons of project benefits with overall business growth;

- other categories of strategic themes selected from the options listed earlier, depending upon the challenges within the company;

- simple scoring models to integrate financial return, strategic value and risk, supported by a structured way to assess strategic value (like Figure 5.7) and a risk scoring system that recognizes the risk of commercial success as well as the risks of delivering the project's solution;

- two or three bubble diagrams to allow the balance of the portfolio to be visualized.

In an organization made up of several business divisions, there will be a difference of emphasis between the divisions and head office. Within each business division, the project investment committee will want to ensure that the business's portfolio has maximum value and the investment committee will want to review detailed evidence of this value through review of:

- NPV and payback periods

- scoring models that integrate NPV, strategic importance and risk.

The investment committee at divisional level will also assess the allocation of investment. This will use:

- strategic themes (balance of expenditure between key strategic goals)

- comparison of the benefits of projects with overall business growth plans

- bubble diagrams to assess balance.

At the group or head office, where the company-wide project investment committee operates, debate will be dominated more by analysis of the expenditure in strategic themes and in gaining a sense that investment is well-balanced across the entire organization:

- strategic themes (balance of expenditure between key business units)

- comparing the benefits of projects with overall business growth plans

- balance of technology investment

- balance of the portfolios across the company.

5 TOOLS FOR PORTFOLIO MANAGEMENT

INTRODUCTION: WHY TOOLS HELP

As portfolio management practices have gained ground in BAU organizations, there has been a parallel growth in the number and variety of tools to support the process. This section offers a perspective on the tools and their use in achieving success in portfolio management. This is a fast-developing and immature market, so my observations keep clear of specific products.

One can see some obvious reasons for the increasing interest in tools. It is essential that the management of a portfolio is undertaken frequently and dynamically to reflect new business imperatives and market conditions. With the complexity of today's businesses and the pace of change in marketplaces, maintaining portfolios manually is onerous and updating becomes a continual workload. If this results in the portfolio management process not being able to react quickly or help with timely 'what-if' analyses, then it will rapidly be discarded as not being a useful tool for management.

The use of what-if modelling and the more complex analytical techniques described above, where we are trying to optimize portfolio performance while recognizing various constraints and interdependencies, tend to require support from software tools.

We can summarize the ways in which tools can be used to support portfolio management in three areas:

- gathering cost, benefits and progress data for each project (project and resource management);

- selecting which set of projects best delivers our strategic goals (strategic alignment and decision support);

- showing the progress, shape and balance of the portfolio of projects (portfolio visualization).

GATHERING INFORMATION

Project and programme management tools are an obvious starting point for the gathering of data that will inform the portfolio management process. These tools should provide key parameters including costs, the use of critical resources, benefits, timescales and risks. Some of these tools will also be able to display aggregate information in a way that supports and informs the analysis of a portfolio. However, these tools cannot be the whole answer to the challenge of describing the portfolio because they do not trap all of the data required for a portfolio debate, being focused upon control of the tasks, cost, benefits and schedule of complex projects.

We must also bear in mind that we are trying to facilitate a discussion by executive management on the strategic alignment of investment. Such audiences do not want or need a huge amount of project data to make their informed decisions; of course they need to see costs, timescales, benefits and risks, but they certainly do not need the same amount of lower-level information as a project or programme manager. So, in my experience, and even if we use project/programme management tools as the source for some information, the best approach is to use simple spreadsheets to present the key project parameters.

This simple approach is particularly appropriate in the initial stages of introducing portfolio management, as the focus will be upon the more significant projects – perhaps the top 20 to 30 in each business division, which might amount to 100 to 200 across a large organization. Prompted by senior management sponsorship, some organizations have introduced very comprehensive systems to gather project information across all projects, but the danger of this approach is that it takes a long time and much effort to gather the information. Some organizations have spent 12 to 18 months gathering information; during such a period one cannot impact the current expenditure on projects and one is likely to lose executive support for the venture.

STRATEGIC ALIGNMENT AND DECISION SUPPORT

The key techniques of strategic alignment focus upon aligning investment with strategic themes or by scoring competing investments with some aggregated measure of strategic value. As a first step, one should use simple presentation means including the map of projects, which I have found to be a most valuable technique to provoke management debate in the early stages of implementing portfolio management. This map can be produced through simple office desktop software. Print such maps at a large scale, on single not multiple pages, to provoke debate by allowing the user to easily see the entire portfolio (and people will put the large-scale maps on office walls, spreading the word and the debate!).

There are some tools now available that reflect this thematic methodology; enterprise programme management and 'professional service automation' (PSA) tools are offering some capabilities here, as well as some niche offerings.

A new range of tools has emerged to support decision-making. These start with the strategic goals of the organization and guide the user to select the set of projects that best supports the goals. The tools consolidate risk, benefits, strategic alignment, dependencies and constraints such as resources and cost, so that the portfolio of projects is optimized. They typically use some form of 'forced pair' analysis and mathematical techniques as the basis for this optimization.

These tools can be purchased on a standalone basis, but they are more commonly sold as a part of a consulting assignment, where the consultancy facilitates a discussion on the relative merits and strategic alignment of various alternative investments.

One of the challenges of using these tools is that they require significant amounts of data for analysis. Sometimes the business finds it hard to describe their real world competitive situation with the clarity and quantification that the analytical tool anticipates and this challenge is amplified by the high degree of uncertainty and rapid change in today's marketplaces.

Hence, while these techniques are attractive, their cost and data-hungry nature will restrict their application. It might be hard to justify this cost and effort in the early days of implementing portfolio management unless there is strong executive mandate or a critical issue facing the organization. An alternative is to pilot the approach within a single business area or to apply it within a large programme, where:

- significant investment is to be made;

- simple benefits techniques might be considered insufficient to guide investment decisions and alternative selections of projects;

- the programme structure can provide the quality of data that the tools require;

- the cost can be clearly defrayed as a part of the programme.

VISUALIZING THE BALANCE OF THE PORTFOLIO

The final area of the application of tools is that of the balance of the portfolio. I have described the graphical techniques earlier, techniques that are typically presented as some form of bubble diagram. This type of output can be produced initially by spreadsheet packages, but these are difficult to prepare and do not lend themselves to frequent updates. These shortcomings have led to a new breed of tools that allow executive users to view the shape and balance of a portfolio of projects, usually as bubble diagrams or tables, as well as to manipulate the data sets more easily.

Some of these visualization tools only portray the portfolio as diagrams, while others allow the association of strategies with projects through a hierarchy (like the decision support tools mentioned above but without the optimization process).

Other visualization tools are primarily aggregators of project information. While they can illustrate the portfolio well they do not really support the alignment to strategic goals.

A STRATEGY FOR USING TOOLS

Market overview

In the past two years there have been some significant trends in the market for project management tools. As often happens with new applications, today's market for portfolio management tools consists of a confusing mix of niche applications with new intellectual content, existing product suites that offer modular extensions of their range to incorporate the vogue functionality and existing applications that are re-badged as something new.

Improvements in traditional project management tools have made them better at aggregating multiple projects and resources, but their core value remains the effective management of project activity on individual projects. Programme management tools take more of an enterprise view by aggregating tasks and resources across multiple projects. Some tend to have more of a bottom-up feel, aggregating project information as opposed to a top-down alignment with strategic goals, but this is an area of fast development.

Professional services automation (PSA) tools have entered the market, focused on the management of resources across multiple projects. They target consultancy-like organizations where project success is governed by the efficient allocation of scarce resources as much as by the task control of each project. Most PSA tools have plans to improve their portfolio management capabilities, which are currently quite basic, but such capabilities do seem to be a natural extension of their products.

The PSA applications are closely related to other enterprise software applications (those that are used for financial control, logistics and human resources). We can expect these tools to progressively acquire portfolio management capabilities. As they are broad-ranging toolsets, already including project management, financial management and accounting, they offer the prospect of closer integration between portfolio or project data and related systems such as budgeting. This could help embed the process of portfolio management more deeply into processes that manage BAU performance.

Niche products have focused upon the new areas of decision support and portfolio visualization and have also started to include programme management and PMO capabilities.

See Figure 5.10 for a high-level analysis of the types of tools currently in and around the portfolio management space. Today (2006) we can see convergence of various tools into the portfolio space – PSA tools, enterprise resource planning applications from major software players, programme and project management tools, and specialist applications. As is usual in such markets, we can expect to see consolidation of these tools and their suppliers over the next two years.

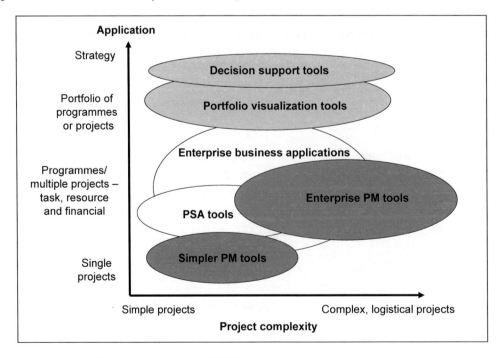

Figure 5.10   The tools market, 2006

Given the pace with which these tools and the market are developing, I will not attempt to provide any form of specific comparison, but valuable comparisons are available from research companies.

A possible strategy for tools

As the information and presentation needs of the various participants in portfolio management will vary widely, I am not convinced that a single application serving all users and information needs is the best solution. Figure 5.11 describes a proposed model that differentiates between users.

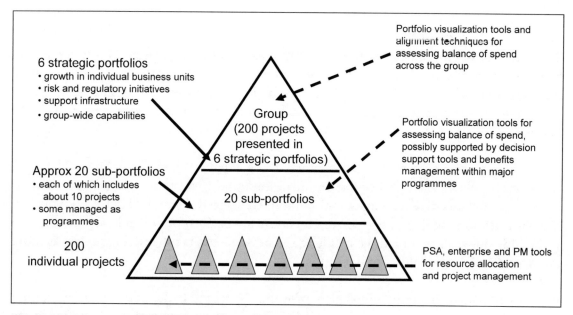

Figure 5.11   A possible strategy for tools

We can start with an assumption that an organization might have up to 200 projects worthy of being tracked in the portfolio (any more becomes unmanageable and the smaller projects should be bundled together as maintenance upgrades/minor works and managed appropriately; often through applying a cap on total expenditure).

Executive level
Assume that the 100–200 projects might be contained within six or so portfolios, each of which therefore has 15 to 30 projects. It is at this level that the senior executive team will want to balance expenditure. This will require tools and techniques that show strategic alignment and help the executive management to visualize the balance of the portfolio.

Business level
In most organizations, each of these six or so portfolios will have a number of sub-portfolios. For example a portfolio of 'becoming a recognized technology leader' might include sub-portfolios for 'low cost processing', 'e-commerce channels' and 'group-wide technology architectures'. We can assume there are three or four sub-portfolios for each portfolio, which is about 20 in all across the organization, and each therefore will contain

from five to ten projects. Some of these sub-portfolios will be managed as programmes, others will not.

At these portfolio and sub-portfolio levels, the debates are less about balance and more about getting the best return on investment. So we could imagine that while the users (business managers and programme teams) will use some strategic alignment and portfolio visualization tools they might also use the more analytical tools for decision support, as an example to decide 'which set of projects best delivers the goal of low-cost processing?' In addition, benefits management techniques are of course of value at these levels.

Project and programme level

Still lower down the model, within programmes or individual projects, the focus will be on traditional project and programme management tools (or the more collaborative tools mentioned in Chapter 3), supplemented by key resource groups using PSA tools or enterprise business applications for an organization-wide view of resources, utilization and costs.

This type of layered model is much more flexible than using one tool for all purposes. It allows each part of the organization to address its own key issues. It does have some obvious disadvantages, including the need to transfer data between tools, but if we are addressing 200 projects in six business areas, each of which has some form of PMO, this does not seem a huge challenge to address. As is often the case, less is more and less data is more informed decisions.

Critically, a layered model also protects against the dangers of an immature marketplace, by not locking the organization into a single tool that might suffer in the competitive market.

6 MAKING IT HAPPEN

INTRODUCTION

This section is structured around the life cycle of implementing the process of portfolio management (a life cycle because the implementation is a project!) and this description is supplemented with descriptions of the key approaches and success criteria that allow the champion of portfolio management to overcome the inevitable challenges in introducing such a change into an organization.

Just as all change projects are subject to politics and resistance to change, introducing portfolio management is subject to politics. Given that the goal of the process is the effective allocation of investment across the organization, one can expect significant political tensions. This section tries to address these tensions by a simple life cycle approach and some practical tips on implementation.

The process can be described as a life cycle with six stages.

STAGE 1 – DECIDE ON MEASURES IMPORTANT TO BUSINESS STRATEGIES

As a precursor to gathering project information, we must first decide the measures that are important to assessing the contribution of each project and hence the portfolio. These measures will cover both the business impact of each project and the performance of each project.

Figure 5.12 shows a typical list of data that could be gathered.

Project name and description
Project objective
Business area
Strategic theme

Project risk score

Strategic value
    benefits > 3 years?
    number of dependent projects
    number of countries impacted
    business impact
    participation/positioning
    competitive advantage
    overall score for strategic value

Process benefit score
Customer benefit score

Start date
Completion date this stage

Costs
    total cash cost
    remaining cash spend
    costs expended before initial flow of benefits

Man-days outstanding
    technology staff
    key business resources

Impact on profit, next three calendar years

Date of initial flow of benefits
Benefit type
    revenue generation
    revenue protection
    cost reduction
    cost avoidance
    mandatory project

Financial benefits per calendar year
Steady state benefits
NPV

Figure 5.12   Data gathering – a list of key project data

The focus on the performance of the project is quite familiar – total cost, the cost still to be spent (that is, the cost that we can influence), the use of scarce resources, the time when benefits will start to flow and the size of the benefits (here shown as both net present value, giving an indication of the net return of the investment over its lifetime and a three-year aggregate of benefits, giving an estimate of the more immediate impact of the project upon the organization).

A risk factor is also included. (Note that, when talking about project risk here, we are ideally referring to the risk of commercial success of the project. Most assessments of project risk in BAU organizations focus primarily upon the risk of delivery of the solution and such assessment techniques will have to be upgraded to address the risk of commercial success if they are to be most useful in portfolio management.)

In Figure 5.12, the other measures address the business impact of the project on the organization. In this example the measures chosen are the same as in Figure 5.7 and tell us something about what this organization considers to be important in its strategic growth. First it has decided to allocate projects to strategic themes, one of the key techniques for assessing the portfolio that has been described earlier. Second, it has included a means of assessing strategic value through a scoring model. This model considers the following elements:

- the longevity of the benefits as a measure of lasting strategic value;

- the number of dependent projects (is this project a platform for future business development, hence offering additional potential value to the organization?);

- the number of countries impacted (in international groups, this measures potential added value and a contribution to standardizing operations);

- business impact (to recognize a desire for some immediate and direct impact);

- participation/positioning (in some businesses it takes considerable time and investment to enter new markets; without recognizing this benefit, initial projects would always receive lower scores than projects in existing markets, hence would not receive investment funds);

- competitive advantage.

This organization is also concerned about the shortage of resources to address multiple opportunities, which can represent an operational risk when BAU resources are re-allocated to work on projects, so it also considers the use of key resources in its portfolio assessment.

In this example, the organization also considers the balance between internally focused and customer-focused investment to be important and wants to assess this balance.

It is important to note that these are quite high-level measures. They must be adequate to assess the part that each project plays within the overall portfolio, but do not make the mistake of setting up processes to gather vast amounts of detailed project information that still cannot inform senior management with a clear picture of how investments are aligned to business goals. We are seeking to engage senior management in an informed debate about priorities and strategic alignment, which is inevitably partly judgmental because it has to include assessments of how markets and competitors will change, based upon imperfect information. The information on project progress and parameters that will be required by project managers is far too detailed for such a debate and the presentation of these types of tools is not user-friendly to senior management teams. So, do not over-engineer the supposed accuracy of the information.

Some time during this stage or the next, the champion of a portfolio management approach will have to seek executive support from the most senior levels in the organization, either by showing some preliminary analysis or posing some provocative questions:

- Why do our projects, across the organization, only deliver x per cent of claimed benefits?

- Why is the aggregate payback period of our projects so long?

- When looked at together, why is it that so many of our projects have business cases with poor financial benefits justified by their supposedly strategic nature?

STAGE 2 – GATHER THE PROJECT INFORMATION

This stage is obviously dependent upon the infrastructure and organization structure that already exists. If there are central programme management offices, then they will be able to provide the information on project performance. So might the technology function, which has a vested interest in the success of portfolio management. The PMOs could also be used to acquire the information on strategic impact, or there might be other teams within the business, including Strategy, Technology or Finance, which could be engaged to provide the information.

It is when we start to gather project information that the first barriers to change can appear:

- Why are we doing this?

- Will it interfere in how I can currently allocate my own investment funds?

- Will it give others a more transparent view of my operations?

- Is this worth the effort?

STAGE 3 – VISUALIZE THE INFORMATION

With a small team (ideally, a small team in each business area to generate local ownership) the data can be analysed and visualized using some of the techniques described earlier.

Take an iterative approach, so that the value of the approach is realized at an early stage and so that techniques and presentation formats can be populated and explored in stages. I recommend the use initially of simple spreadsheets to collate key project parameters, with the use of:

- a map of projects aligned with strategic themes;

- a view of how investment is split between revenue growth and cost reduction;

- aggregated benefits and costs shown by both strategic theme and business area;

- a scoring model of strategic value;

- one or two means of describing the balance of the portfolio – perhaps risk plotted against reward or how investments are allocated between internal- and customer-focused goals.

STAGE 4 – CREATE A MANAGEMENT DEBATE

Even with the initial analysis, there will be interesting conclusions that can be taken to senior management for discussion. Management will wish to contribute not only to any initial assessment of the portfolio, but to the choice and ranking of the measures of strategic value (some of which is defensive behaviour by individual managers looking to adjust the debate in their favour). It is at this time that visible, senior sponsorship is first required, so that the discussion can be progressed objectively.

There are two goals to this stage: to engage senior management on the initial discussion of the current investment in projects and to also decide the ongoing governance process that will be adopted to manage the portfolio. Each of these goals will require that we overcome political tensions, 'turf wars' and vested interests.

Discuss the current process that is used to guide investment in projects

The engagement of senior management will of course be handled in a manner that reflects the unique culture of each organization. Key factors to consider will be:

- existing decision-making processes (in particular existing processes for project investment, but also related processes including how the annual budget is set, how BAU performance is measured and managed and how budgets or forecasts are varied during the year to reflect changed business circumstances);

- the planning horizon that is used at the organization, bearing in mind the volatility of markets and the organization's appetite for short- and long-term investment;

- the decision-making culture in the organization (so that the approach used for managing the portfolio will feel like a natural evolution of existing decision-making processes – how formal a committee structure is required, how collegiate is the decision-making in general within the organization?).

Try to use existing processes and governance structures as building blocks for the process, portraying the process as an evolutionary step that applies new techniques and hence better informs the processes that are already in place:

- existing processes for managing the strategic agenda;

- existing PMOs (likely to be critical anyway to the gathering of project information);

- existing project and programme management methodologies (for example, how projects are approved and how stages are used on projects). A standardized project management process will prove essential to managing the portfolio;

- existing committees for project approval or performance management.

Use the scoring models to promote debate about the strategic value of individual projects. This debate will initially focus more on the model itself, as owners of projects will naturally wish to see their projects as well aligned to strategy and ranked highly. Let this debate happen; it engages management teams and builds ownership as they refine the scoring models.

Find ways in which the proposed process will reduce bureaucracy and increase the level of delegation across the organization. The positioning here is that, in recognition of the structured process for managing investment that will be in place across the organization, greater autonomy can be provided to individual business areas. Consider increasing the approval levels for projects as a measure of this.

Decide the future process that will be adopted to manage the portfolio

The ongoing process must also be designed and agreed by a number of stakeholders. As with the engagement of senior management, this process will of course reflect the unique culture and needs of each organization. However, we can again prescribe some key aspects of the process that will apply in all cases.

You cannot have debate about priorities without having a scarce resource to force the prioritization. A scarce resource, using the definition adopted by economists, is one that has finite supply. It acts as a form of common currency across projects. Choose the scarce resource that works best in your organization and be prepared to change it as the portfolio approach matures. It could be cash investment costs, manpower in specific skill areas or the impact upon profit and loss account or balance sheet.

Consider carefully how the proposed process will achieve a balance between a regular assessment of the alignment and balance of the portfolio and the re-appraisal of projects at Stage Review gates (with associated stop/go decisions). If the Stage Reviews dominate the process, then we can maximize financial performance of the portfolio but do we have the right blend of projects and do we react fast enough to changes in the external market? If the portfolio review dominates, then our holistic support of the strategic agenda should be strong, but are we tough enough on under-performing projects? Ideally, we should have a balance between the two approaches, but the right emphasis must reflect the needs of the business: its decision-making culture, market volatility, risk appetite and investment capacity.

Build promised benefits into business budgets. This is a critical success factor for the ongoing support (and embedding into BAU) of the process. The approach is simple in principle and depicted in Figure 5.13.

The costs and claimed benefits of each project investment are added into business budgets, which already include organic growth, to give a total view of business growth.

Why is this approach so important? It provides ultimate accountability for the return on investment. It also has the benefits of:

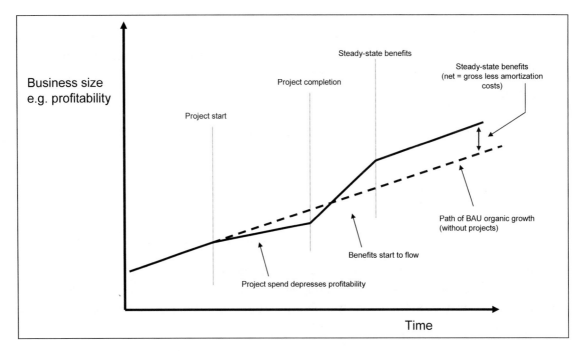

Figure 5.13   Building benefits into business budgets

- forcing realism on the benefits claimed in project proposals, as the benefits will simply be added into the business targets for the executive making the proposal;

- overcoming the reluctance of organizations to track project benefits. The approver of the investment is in effect saying to the proposer, 'You can undertake whatever benefits tracking you like and whatever is appropriate to the project and your business. You have claimed some benefits in return for an investment and I am going to hold you accountable for the benefits as a part of your BAU business targets.'

Building benefits into business budgets is less easy in practice; it is often a matter of judgment to segregate between BAU growth and the impact of projects. In some cases, it is not obvious whether an activity is BAU or a project; for example, should incremental marketing spend be classed as a project and assessed in competition with other investment projects or is it simply a part of ongoing BAU expenditure? But the principle of building the benefits into budgets is critical to success. Just as we have discussed in Chapter 3, where embedded project skills were proposed as the most effective focus for leading BAU organizations, the approach of building benefits into budgets promotes the embedded nature of the projects themselves; projects are not, after all, 'outside BAU' but are the means by which we change the state of BAU, hence 'inside BAU'.

Make sure the process is focused upon business projects. One damaging perception of projects (as described in Chapter 2) is that they are 'technology projects' or 'owned by technology'. Nearly all projects in BAU organizations are business projects within which there are significant technology components. Business projects have business benefits. A few projects, for example the upgrade of core technology infrastructure, will be sponsored within the Technology function and they will be accountable for the benefits, but the vast majority of projects must be seen as business ventures, enabled by technology. A danger of the focus upon technology (as it is one of the key drivers for the portfolio process) is that commentators have started talking about 'IT portfolio management'; while the technology community must of course assess that its own contribution to the strategic agenda is balanced and optimized, we must not make the mistake of delegating the management of business-driven projects to the Technology function.

Position the process as a part of BAU performance management of the organization. Project investment might be a specialist area, with its own set of techniques, but from the earliest stages we want it to be perceived as inside BAU, a driver of business performance rather than separate. It should be presented as a subset of the general approach that the organization takes to manage its overall business performance. This has implications for the governance of the process, roles and responsibilities. If the Finance function undertakes the performance management process across the organization (the normal situation) then it is desirable that this function also leads the investment process for projects.

One process usually has pre-eminence in all organizations – setting the annual budget. It is critical that we establish, from an early stage, how the portfolio process can be integrated into the budget cycle (back again to our theme of becoming a part of BAU as soon as possible). A key, early success will be to extract all project bids which have historically been hidden within BAU budgets, and then to hold a management debate to set priorities; agreed projects are then input back into the business budgets. This process forces an early trial of prioritization and will give the portfolio process some credibility and standing at an early stage.

STAGE 5 – IMPLEMENTATION

Particularly in the early stages, describe the process primarily in terms of its benefits to each operating unit/division, not to group/head office. The initial focus is that each operating unit should use a portfolio management process so that it can make the best use of its own investment capacity.

The group centre should assess its own investments with similar rigour before starting to analyse the portfolios of business units. Optimizing the portfolio across the organization can come later – this is both practical (because it is of limited value to try to optimize the overall portfolio if each part is not optimized) and politically expedient as it prevents the process being seen as a means for head office to reallocate investment between divisions (which will only lead to opacity, not transparency).

Similarly, promote the formation of project investment committees most visibly at business levels.

Look for some early successes from the process. Obvious targets here are that the initial analysis could find projects that are weakly aligned to strategic goals and are therefore candidates for cancellation. There could also be projects in different divisions that have similar goals or are building overlapping deliverables, hence there are opportunities for consolidation. The use of scoring models could provide some early opportunities to reassess priorities, use fewer resources or accelerate the flow of benefits. Most industry surveys of portfolio management have shown significant benefits here.

Less obvious, but of potential benefit, is the opportunity for efficiencies across the portfolio. As an example, procurement practices on projects in BAU organizations are typically not well integrated across the organization, certainly not as well integrated as the procurement for BAU items that are directly used in the production process or general management. Looking for efficiencies such as volume discounting or better predictability of orders with key suppliers can be a valuable and highly visible early success.

An alternative approach to generating early benefits and gaining ongoing executive support (just as project managers use on any type of change project) is to select one business area as a pilot for the portfolio management approach.

STAGE 6 – ITERATIVE IMPROVEMENT

As the reader will have gathered from this chapter, portfolio management might be quite simple in concept, but its implementation needs careful thought, a master plan or roadmap to guide the journey and strong business sponsorship. The portfolio management process allocates resources and funds (which equals the allocation of organizational and personal power) and hence is inevitably a deeply political process. It seeks to change people's behaviour, always a risky venture. So expectations must be set and carefully managed.

Not all aspects of the process will work well the first time and some political barriers will not be overcome immediately. In many cases the work will have to be carried out at a pace that is slow enough that senior managers start to request the next stage, instead of it being imposed upon them. The same careful pace applies to the use of tools, which will be regarded as a bureaucratic overhead if proposed too soon, but can be supplied as a response to senior managers' requests; if the champion of portfolio management shows patience, other senior managers will start to push the process forwards.

As mentioned above, do not become a slave to perfect data, and ensure that all participants agree with this (or the process will get bogged down in arguments about data quality).

NOTES ON THE CHANGE PROCESS

Usually, when introducing new approaches to organizations, we hold in high regard the value of senior management sponsorship to give direction and support to the project. This senior management support is then used to communicate very visibly the goals of the project and the nature of the changes that each affected stakeholder can expect to see. This is classical change management.

However, this is not the only way to create change. People will change behaviour if they are informed by new information, and the introduction of portfolio management is an example where, provided with the right information in a well-structured and well-presented manner, people will change behaviour. If a senior manager is presented with project proposals on a standalone basis, he or she will react to them on a standalone basis. But if shown portfolio information, the same manager will start to ask about trade-offs and relative strategic value; this is only natural.

This approach takes careful analysis and planning (and patience). If applied through low-key communications with those directly involved, not high visibility communications, it is a classical 'stealth project' as described in Chapter 3.

In line with this subtle approach, it pays to think carefully about the name that is given to the initiative to implement portfolio management. If it sounds too complex or academic, one might want to use a simpler title – 'project selection process' or 'investment management process' as examples.

Chief executive	We will spend our money more wisely, with better selection of projects based upon their contribution to strategic objectives
	We can more easily drive business benefits out of the investments
	We can regularly align expenditure with your strategic agenda (more responsive to market changes)
	We can help you increase the growth rate of the business
Chief finance officer	Better use of investment funds
	Focus our resource on the most relevant projects
	Kill low value projects earlier so they do not drain resources
	Show the contribution of IT more clearly, prioritize effort
	Promote accountability for the delivery of business benefits
Senior managers	Realistic benefits in business cases, better project proposals
	You will get option to review, not a rubber stamp
	Your challenge will add value
	You will get more autonomy in return for following the process and accepting that funds will be allocated where they generate the best strategic return
	Regular review of project progress lets you manage risk better
Project managers	Gives you a better business context for the project (which means executive support and helps you make better decisions)
	Gives you better metrics from previous projects
	Helps you gain project resources without the current chaos
	Helps strategic suppliers to forecast workload demands

Figure 5.14   Key sales messages for portfolio management

The approach might be subtle, but we still have to sell it to stakeholders, based upon a clear set of value propositions. Figure 5.14 shows some of the key messages of added value through the process, tailored to different audiences.

NOTES ON KEY CONTRIBUTORS

PMOs have a natural role to play in the portfolio management process. As we have discussed in Chapter 3, PMOs should have an overview of the various projects underway and, as we move to the embedded models for skills, they have a role in providing best practice to project teams, which will allow them to check that new projects are following practices that will support the portfolio process.

A key issue to consider is whether the PMO has the right skills to facilitate the portfolio process (with its strategic emphasis) or whether others should manage the process, informed by the PMO. The transition from a PMO being a tracker of project progress or centre of excellence for project management disciplines to a portfolio manager is no small matter and each organization must consider if this is desirable and achievable.

From the nature of the portfolio management process, it is clear that the process will affect Finance, Strategy, and Technology functions. With our focus on embedding the process within BAU processes for investment and managing business performance, the Finance or Strategy functions might have a much closer engagement, perhaps undertaking the role of secretariat to the investment committees. The correct involvement of these functions in the process will be critical to success.

NOTES ON THE IMPACT UPON PROJECT AND PROGRAMME MANAGEMENT PROCESSES

The portfolio process focuses on how we manage the portfolio of projects and hence how we select the best set of projects to support our strategic agenda. So whatever existing approach applies to delivering projects and managing change is largely unaffected.

But there will be some changes. First of all, the use of the portfolio process will affect how projects are approved. The use of the Concept Paper, Project Request and Stage Review, or some version of these, must be integrated into the methodologies for project and programme management. The greater attention to delivering major projects as stages will affect how some projects are planned and subdivided. It will also encourage greater discipline in the use of formal project life cycles. The regular review of the portfolio will drive the delivery of benefits and encourage project teams to estimate costs and benefits with more care.

With a more rigorous process for investment and the knowledge that the process will allow the ongoing risk of the projects to be managed, companies can opt for simpler approval documentation.

This ability to progressively manage risk means that companies can also consider giving greater delegated authority to individual business units; the level of expenditure that causes specific group/head office review of Project Requests can be raised.

Essentially the group or head office is pulling back to focus on portfolio review rather than the review of individual projects and programmes. This is a more mature approach and reflects that in BAU organizations there is typically a high level of accountability and project funding residing within each division.

Finally, the clearer view of the strategic contribution of each project will result in a more informed management debate, reducing the time wasted in ad hoc reviews and debates about projects.

7 CONCLUSIONS

To summarize, programme management disciplines can be key to driving a benefits culture, as well as giving us control over the more complex initiatives. But benefits are not the complete answer to the strategic alignment of our investments in projects and there are constraints to the success of programme management, arising from culture and behaviour in the real world.

I believe that progressing to a portfolio management approach can improve the quality of strategic alignment because it provides management teams with a number of ways to appraise their investments. It optimizes investment against strategic goals whereas other techniques, including benefits management, can be considered as narrower views of the investment challenge. This more holistic, responsive approach to strategic alignment seems right, to me, in today's increasingly volatile business world.

The concept of considering initiatives or investments as some form of portfolio is not new. In the world of business strategy and marketing, the 1960s saw the use of the Boston Matrix for appraising business strategy across a portfolio of product areas and the Ansoff Matrix was developed as a means of analysing how an organization could balance and direct its efforts on the launch of products into existing or new markets.

In the 1950s, Harry Markowitz had developed his 'modern portfolio theory', mathematical approaches for managing risk and return across a portfolio of investments.

The approaches that I have summarized in this chapter are not new either. They have been used over the past two decades and a number of the portfolio appraisal techniques have also been around for a number of years.

Strangely though, even in companies that use portfolio approaches for product development, they have only recently started to make the transition into the world of business change projects and programmes. It is perhaps no accident that some of the recent enthusiasts are found in large financial services companies, where the concepts of financial portfolio management are already well established.

It is not just in financial services that the use of portfolio management is growing fast, prompted by the drivers mentioned earlier.

Thus far, though, the project and programme management profession has largely ignored these techniques. Portfolios are often considered as some loose association of projects that exist outside of the purist model of a number of programmes equating to the change agenda of the organization.

The project and programme management profession should start to consider portfolio management more seriously; think of it not as a conflict with programme management, but as complementary. Consider it as a means of overcoming the issues that are prevalent in using programme management within BAU organizations and as a way to provide an improved linkage of projects with strategy, hence one that can help our profession to add further value to business activity through the concerted delivery of change projects.

CHAPTER 6

Conclusions

CHANGE AND BAU ORGANIZATIONS

In this book I have pursued a number of themes that apply to the management of projects in non-traditional areas, in particular where we are managing the delivery of business change projects that we would describe as 'soft' when compared with the 'hard' projects that were the focus of our attention when the discipline of project management was born and matured. These themes have included:

- The improvement of project performance is best achieved by a framework of measures that includes a balance of process discipline and personal skills.

- The methodologies applied for the delivery of softer projects should better reflect the importance of project design, project governance and processes for the management of the business case and business change.

- While both business skills and project management skills are essential to the success of any project, we should be giving greater emphasis to the provision of business skills than is typically the case.

- The divisions that are created between project, programme and portfolio management are often exaggerated and we should focus more upon the commonalities across them, recognizing them as a continuum rather than discrete approaches. The use of benefits techniques and stages to reduce risk were described earlier as examples.

I have, though, proposed that many of the problems in improving project performance in softer projects come not from the projects but from the nature of the organizations in which they are taking place. These organizations are not dedicated to the delivery of projects. They are dedicated to the day-by-day, business-as-usual management of production or processing activities and the daily provision of services to their customers. They need to have business change projects, to move from one BAU steady-state to another, improving their efficiency, capacity and competitiveness, but the projects are a means to an end, not the end itself.

While the projects are important to the pursuit of the organization's strategy, they cannot be as central to the executive agenda in a BAU organization as they are in a projectized one. Building a project delivery capability and successfully delivering projects is always going to be a challenging task in such organizations.

A BUSINESS ISSUE FOR THE PROJECT MANAGEMENT PROFESSION

Most research on the delivery of projects assumes that the host organization is projectized. Even when change projects in BAU organizations are the subject of the research, there seems to be an assumption that they will be delivered through imposing a largely projectized approach onto the host.

This projectized approach has its merits and has produced positive results. Many organizations can claim that they have improved the performance of their projects by noticeable amounts through the application of project management disciplines and the nurturing of project management skills. However, I have observed a growing concern in such organizations that, after a promising start, the rate of improvement has slowed and champions of project management are finding it more difficult to maintain executive sponsorship for the competency of project management.

I hope that this book will contribute to a wider debate on how we seek the next stage of improvement in project delivery.

As I have described more than once in this book, I believe that our project management profession has some responsibility for the loss of enthusiasm for project management. In transferring our disciplines to BAU organizations we should have considered the nature of these BAU organizations more carefully; our techniques have not always been in tune with the nature of the host organization and we have not tailored our techniques sufficiently to address this. But I would rather build upon the many successes to date, by taking the discussion onwards.

Over and above the tailoring of existing approaches to better suit BAU organizations, we must start to think of the challenge of managing change projects in these organizations in a very different way. There are three rallying cries to this different way:

- We will find a way to position projects differently, as 'inside BAU' not 'outside BAU'. We want organizations to define BAU as encompassing a blend of operational, day-to-day activities and those project activities devoted to improving the status quo.

- We do not want projects to be perceived as special events or as tasks to be conducted through some specialist black art.

- We will focus upon 'project delivery', being the object of the exercise, not 'project management', being the technique that helps us along the journey.

EMBEDDING A CAPABILITY IN THE ORGANIZATION

With these rallying cries in mind, this book investigated in Chapter 3 how we could improve the capability of an organization to deliver projects. Chapter 3 proposed that we would make significant improvements through applying a project management framework, but then went further.

I proposed that we must change the focus of the framework in BAU organizations and concentrate much more on the development of an embedded skill; one that is provided to a very wide range of staff who are engaged occasionally on the projects that improve the business area in which they work. This will be a significant change of direction for most organizations and has implications for how those project management professionals who regularly participate in projects should conduct themselves and be deployed.

EMBEDDING PROJECTS IN THE ORGANIZATION'S STRATEGIC AGENDA

Chapters 4 and 5 have developed another aspect of embedding project delivery deeply within the organization. Chapter 5 concluded that the portfolio management approach will complement existing disciplines of project and/or programme management and allow us to optimize project investments against strategic goals. It does this in a way that recognizes that the strategic contribution of projects is wider than an aggregation of project benefits. It portrays its conclusions in a way that is in tune with the needs of executive management in BAU organizations.

The use of portfolio approaches is not yet widespread, but many organizations are taking their first steps along this path. The path is risky, since it addresses processes that are inevitably highly political, but the prizes are huge.

The obvious prize is that if we serve executive management well with strategic advice, the organization can make better use of its investment funds. This is a laudable goal in itself, but there is also a prize for those who champion the cause of project delivery in the organization. Because the process will demonstrate (in a clearer way than our specialist discipline has done to date) exactly how the various projects are delivering parts of the strategic agenda, we can obtain much greater executive support for the competency of project delivery and can therefore look to create a sustained improvement in performance of projects across the enterprise.

EXECUTIVE SUPPORT

A campaign to improve project delivery requires time and a steady progression of capabilities. We call this progression 'maturity' and this is a subject attracting much interest at present in the project management profession. At the top of Figure 6.1, I have presented a typical depiction of a maturity model (a number of which are available

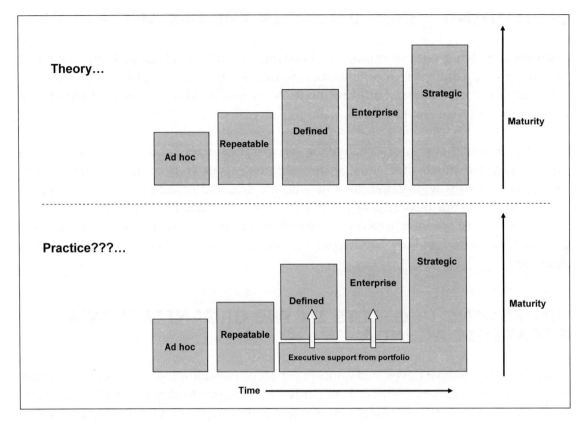

Figure 6.1   A new view of project management maturity

in research papers). My version focuses on how the capability becomes progressively better defined and then applied across the enterprise, with consistency and then for strategic advantage. The specific steps are less important than the concept of the progression in maturity.

I propose that most campaigns to improve project delivery, if they are based upon a simplistic model of transporting projectized project management approaches to BAU organizations, will lose momentum in the third and fourth stages of maturity. What they need is a fresh impetus and that impetus is to position project delivery very centrally as a competency critical to the execution of the portfolio of investments that makes up much of the organization's strategic agenda. Hence, my version of a maturity progression is depicted at the bottom of Figure 6.1; moving at the right time to a portfolio view is critical to energizing executive support and so is critical to a sustainable campaign to improve project delivery.

In combination, the embedded skill of project delivery will best suit BAU organizations and will receive sustained corporate support if the most senior levels of management recognize the projects' contribution as an integral, embedded part of the strategic agenda.

THE RIGHT TIME FOR A FRESH APPROACH

I believe that there is a growing realization that BAU organizations need closer analysis as hosts for project delivery. There are also a number of drivers for a fresh look at this time. Taking financial service companies as an example, these drivers include:

- *The increasing attention being placed upon good corporate governance, now reinforced by legislation.* Where projects represent a significant part of the cost base, there will be an expectation that similar controls and executive oversight are in place for investment decisions and the subsequent management of projects as is in place for BAU activity.

- *The imperative for banks and other financial service businesses to manage operational risks as efficiently as credit and market risks.* If not managed properly, the aggregate collection of projects can represent an operational risk as it diverts or stretches BAU resource and therefore increases the level of risk elsewhere in the business. Over-dependency on outsourced operations or key suppliers for project delivery might not be identified if it is spread across the portfolio and this will lead to further operational risks.

- *Staying with operational risk, there is also an argument that any cost and schedule over-runs on projects could be considered as representing operational losses* (are they any different to those losses caused by failed customer transactions, for both are due to a process that has not operated properly?). Financial services regulators are increasing their focus on operational losses within their supervisory regimes and the measures that they expect organizations to take to address them will have significant consequences.

- *The current emphasis on better defining the core competencies that will allow the organization to compete in today's complex markets.* If we are to embed the skill of project delivery more deeply in the organization, what better time to promote it than when there is already a focus on the skills that allow the organization to innovate and react with the speed needed in today's business world?

These are key business issues and consequently they are high up the agenda of chief executives and boards. The timing has never been better to promote new approaches that improve project governance and manage project risk.

ISSUES FOR FURTHER CONSIDERATION

I hope that this book contributes to a wider debate about the best way to improve project delivery in BAU organizations. These are early days in this debate. I believe that it is a debate that can be accelerated through the use of the embedded approaches in this book, but I also recognize that there will be many implications of the embedded approach that will have to be considered in the context of each organization. Here are some areas for further research and thought.

Who should sponsor the improvement of project delivery in a BAU organization? With the emphasis on embedding the skill of project delivery and embedding the projects within the strategic agenda, it might be appropriate to use the Human Resources and Strategy functions as sponsors (rather than the Finance and Technology functions' sponsorship that has typically been the case). Will this work in practice? Will it work in your organization?

If we adopt a more subtle approach to this embedded skill, how will the champion of project management receive due visibility and reward for achievements? If the role is invisible, how can we get experienced staff to fill it, for anyone worth the role will have ambition and require recognition?

With the emphasis on business leadership of projects, how will we prevent the role of the project manager being relegated to someone who simply manages the project control function on the project? This would certainly make the role much less attractive to anyone with advanced project management skills, but it would also open up risks to the project. As we know from experience, if the project manager does not take considerable interest in the business case then the project team delivers in a blinkered fashion that ignores changes in the business.

If we portray the discipline of project management too much as an enabling skill, then the specialists will lose the power to influence events on projects, being classified as technical advisors, no more.

So, plenty to discuss, but I hope that this book is a step along the journey!

Project Management – Minimum Control Standards

This appendix sets out the minimum control standards to be applied to business change projects. The standards are intended to guide sponsors, accountable executives and project managers as to the minimum level of management discipline that is acceptable on projects.

Separate documents describe how projects are classified by level of risk and how the governance, assurance and staffing are enhanced for the riskier projects (see Appendix 4).

Standards and processes have been defined for the following areas:

1. Project life cycle and approvals

2. Standard project roles and responsibilities

3. Project governance

4. Business case and benefits

5. Business acceptance of change

6. Project initiation, planning and staging

7. Project monitoring and control

8. Financial management

9. Quality management

10. People management

11. Procurement.

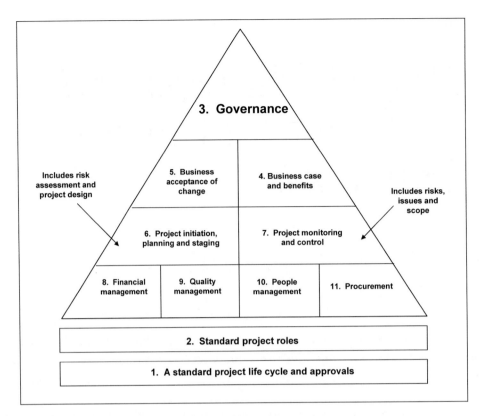

Figure A1.1   Project management process

Table A1.1   Project management processes

Standard	Minimum Requirement	Person Responsible
Project life cycle and approvals		
A project is a temporary set of activities. It has an identified beginning and end. During the intervening period the project passes through distinct stages and these comprise the project life cycle	• Projects must seek formal approval, at an early time, through a Concept Paper, which describes the rationale for the project and its strategic alignment. A Concept Paper must be completed where the anticipated cost of the overall project is £xxx or whatever is the stipulated limit set by the relevant project investment committee	Accountable executive
The management of the project through its life cycle is the fundamental difference between the role of a project manager and a manager of BAU activities. This difference highlights the specific skill set and attributes to be displayed when acting in the role of a project manager	• The project must follow the company's standard life cycle, which comprises a number of phases	Project manager
	• Following feasibility or detailed planning, as appropriate, the project must return to seek full funding approval through a Project Request	Accountable executive
	• The transition from one phase of the life cycle to the next and the eventual closure of project activity must be agreed formally by the project steering commmittee (PSC)	Accountable executive
	• Where there are valid reasons for a subsequent phase to start before the previous phase has been fully completed, this must be based upon a clear assessment of benefits, costs and risks and must be approved by the PSC	Accountable executive
	• At each phase transition there must be a review of the project structure, resources and management methods that are appropriate to the next phase; the costs for these methods being included within the budget	Project manager
	• A post implementation review is to be prepared to summarize the performance of the project against its objectives. The post implementation review should include the lessons learned during the project. The output from the review should be presented to key stakeholders and archived where it can be of value to future projects	Accountable executive

Table A1.1   *continued*

Standard	Minimum Requirement	Person Responsible
Standard project roles and responsibilities		
As project and programme organizations are temporary, it is important that roles and responsibilities within them are clearly specified and agreed	• For all projects, a sponsor (S), accountable executive (AE) and project manager (PM) must be appointed. For low risk projects, the S and the AE may be the same person • Responsibilities of the S, AE and PM must be documented	Sponsor Sponsor
Three key roles are expected as the core management team for the project	• The AE must ascertain the appropriateness of the proposed project manager, including relevant prior project experience and training	Accountable executive
	• The AE and PM are responsible for ensuring that the appropriate advice/guidance is received from technology, finance, legal, tax and other relevant internal functions	Accountable executive and project manager
	• The PSC is responsible for all policy decisions relating to the project (see also separate standards on governance)	Sponsor
	• The AE is accountable for the delivery of benefits specified in the project request	Accountable executive
	• The PM is responsible for the delivery of the project's solution	Project manager

Table A1.1 *continued*

Standard	Minimum Requirement	Person Responsible
Project governance		
Effective project governance is key to the success of business change projects. Governance will include a formal process for steering the project	• The PSC must meet at least once every two months. Attendees will include S (Chair), AE, PM and key business stakeholders	Sponsor to set up and chair the PSC

The PSC is responsible for all policy decisions in relation to the project. They consider what must be done in terms of cost, quality and time	• The agenda must cover:
	  – latest high level schedule
	  – review of progress, including major milestone tracking
	  – the top five risks (relevant risks must also be passed on to the appropriate BAU risk committees for their parallel management)
	  – a review of project financials covering actuals to date, forecast to date and forecast through to project completion
	  – scope changes
		Project manager

In addition to regular reporting of project progress, all stakeholders will need focused communication on their needs and issues (see also standards for business acceptance of change)	• The PSC must formally approve the project management plan (PMP), other key project documents and phase transitions	Sponsor
Projects are also subject to governance from programme structures and/or the project investment committee	• The PSC must ensure that the health of the project is reviewed at appropriate times during the life cycle. This could include independent reviews and audit involvement (see Appendix 4)	Sponsor
	• Except on low-risk projects, the PM will chair a Project Working Committee to direct day-to-day activities with the project team and affected functional managers	Accountable executive/ project manager
	• The project must submit a clear statement of progress, risks and benefits to the portfolio management process, governed by the project investment committee	

Table A1.1   *continued*

Standard	Minimum Requirement	Person Responsible
Business case and benefits		
The business case of the project describes its investment costs and return on investment. Benefits management of a project provides management with a structured approach to realizing the forecasted benefits, both financial and non-financial, as measured against the approved financial budget and other key performance indicators (KPIs)	• The project's business case will include both financial and non-financial benefits, and the means by which these benefits will be measured must be included in the Project Request	Accountable executive
	• The financial benefits must be included in the project's cashflow and P&L statements	Accountable executive

	• A benefits realization plan must be formulated to:
	  – identify all the expected business benefits and their nature
	  – outline the baseline KPIs to be measured
	  – state how the benefits will be achieved
	  – state how the benefits are to be tracked, specifying cost centres, with sign off from respective managers
	  – include a benefits realization timeline
		Accountable executive/project manager

The benefits information is important to evaluate the success of a project or programme against the original business case included in the Project Request	• The financial benefits must be included in the project scorecard produced for each project in accordance with the reporting cycle of the sponsor's business unit	Accountable executive/project manager
See Appendix 2 for guidance notes on benefits management	• A benefits review report must be produced at appropriate milestones in the project. This will typically be aligned with a Stage Review. The report should clearly show the projected realization of both financial and non-financial benefits measured against the baseline KPIs and financial benefits budget, as outlined in the benefits realization plan	Accountable executive
	• At the completion of the project or programme, a benefits review must be undertaken	Sponsor
	• The financial benefits must continue to be tracked against the original business case or added into BAU business targets, whichever is the most meaningful approach	Sponsor/accountable executive

Table A1.1 *continued*

Standard	Minimum Requirement	Person Responsible
Business acceptance of change		
The success of a project is ultimately dependent upon the willingness and capability of the business to accept for use the product or solution delivered and therefore to realize the forecast benefits	• The impact of change upon the organization must be explicitly considered within the design of the project. This analysis must include a structured assessment of the project's stakeholders. Stakeholders are not limited to those users directly affected by the project; they include functions and managers whose opinions or requirements must be recognized either in the project solution or in the conduct of the project	Project manager
The effective management of change requires the careful management of all stakeholders, the engagement of affected staff in the objectives of the project, and clear communications of the project's progress and intentions	• This analysis will result in a change strategy, developed in the detailed planning phase, that must be included within the Project Management Plan or, if complexity requires, a separate document. The AE must approve this strategy	Accountable executive
See Appendix 3 for guidance notes on managing change and stakeholders	• The change strategy must cover the appropriate management of key stakeholders. This will require, at a minimum, regular communications with these stakeholders, but could also indicate that other actions are required in order to achieve support or desired behaviour from stakeholders	Accountable executive/ project manager
	• At an early phase of the project, the PM must confirm the basis upon which the deliverables of the project will be accepted. This should be with the full involvement of the business users	Project manager
	• A dialogue on acceptance must be maintained throughout the project, including reviewing the potential impact of any scope changes	Project manager
	• The process of gaining business acceptance will be governed by procedures for testing and demonstrating the quality of the solution. Procedures will include final approval by the PSC	Sponsor/accountable executive
	• Acceptance and putting into use can be granted incrementally, but only with the approval of the PSC	Accountable executive

Table A1.1   *continued*

Standard	Minimum Requirement	Person Responsible
Project initiation, planning and staging		
Project initiation and planning is the process of defining and documenting all management aspects of a project, from initiation to closure The result is a Project Management Plan (PMP) and formal request for funding The PMP serves as a means by which the project manager can communicate to all parties how the project will be run The PMP might be supported with a sub-plan describing particular requirements of the project (for example, the technology deliverables)	• A Project Management Plan (PMP) should be prepared for all projects and conform to the standard template including: – statement of work – work breakdown structure – project team structure – solution approach – resource requirements (includes how they overlap with BAU) – management methods including time, cost, scope, quality – change management and acceptance plans • Initially within the feasibility phase, and then reviewed in the detailed planning phase, there must be an appraisal of the risk profile of the project and this must be used to put in place an appropriate governance and control regime for the project	Project manager Accountable executive/project manager
	• The PMP must include the design of the project's organization structure to demonstrate how it addresses the challenges of the project including: – its work breakdown structure – key risks – how the project should be segregated from BAU – the need to manage change in varied parts of the organization – the contract strategy – governance	Project manager
The funding request – Project Request (PR) – is required to obtain appropriate approvals for the project to proceed and for financial resources to be allocated directly to the project. Project requests will not be considered for approval unless accompanied by a robust PMP Large projects will be subdivided into stages to reduce risks and accelerate benefits. See guidance in Appendix 5	• The PR must be prepared in accordance with the standard templates. It must explicitly state how the project supports business strategy • Major projects must consider dividing the full project into a number of delivery stages, each of which delivers some tangible business benefit. This approach reduces both project risk and the financial exposure before the project generates a return	Accountable executive/project manager Accountable executive/project manager

Table A1.1   *continued*

Standard	Minimum Requirement	Person Responsible
Project monitoring and control		
Timely and accurate reporting is essential in ensuring stakeholders are kept fully informed on the progress of the project and to draw involvement from relevant stakeholders in resolution of project conflicts, concerns, issues and risks	• For major projects, at the minimum, progress reports must be produced and issued to members of the PSC and other key stakeholders, before each PSC meeting and in accordance with the organization's reporting calendar	Accountable executive/project manager
	• Progress reports must follow the standard template for reporting of milestones, costs, benefits, risks and issues	Project manager
	• Every project must maintain a 'risk and issue' register that is monitored and updated on a regular basis	Project manager
	• Where relevant the project will also maintain a dependencies log/database to manage external dependencies that will impact progress.	Project manager
	• Every project must have in place a change control process that manages project scope. Material changes in scope, quality, cost or schedule must be documented and approved by the AE	Project manager
	• All reporting to external parties, for example regulators, auditors, and so on, is to be formally managed via a set timetable and through designated personnel	Project manager
	• All formal meetings, for example working committee and PSC meetings, must be formally documented with minutes issued to participants and key stakeholders	

Table A1.1 *continued*

Standard	Minimum Requirement	Person Responsible
Financial management		
The financial management of a project provides the team with a timely status of committed and forecasted expenditure against the approved budget The information on the financial status of a project is an important tool for management decision making, and allows the PSC to monitor the validity of the original business case	• Following the standard format, a cashflow and profit and loss statement must be included in the PR	Accountable executive
	• Company accounting policy and guidelines must be followed at all times as detailed in the appropriate accounting policy manual	Project manager
	• The project budget must accurately reflect all costs, including the costs of internal staff	Project manager
	• Project budgets must include contingency. This is to be defined in relation to project risk and managed by the project manager, with approval to use authorized by the PSC	Project manager
	• The taxation aspects of any expenditure must be included in the total cost	Project manager
	• All project costs must be tracked against the budget in the PR. Any forecast excesses of 10 per cent on individual cost items must be reported with reasons to the PSC in order to provide early warning of budget overruns	Accountable executive/project manager

Table A1.1 *continued*

Standard	Minimum Requirement	Person Responsible
Quality management		

Quality management consists of quality control and quality assurance
 	
Quality control is the process of monitoring and evaluating deliverables to ensure compliance with specifications
 	
Quality assurance is the process that provides the confidence that a project will deliver to expectation. This is most important in planning and monitoring
	• A quality management plan (QMP) must be produced either separately or as part of the PMP. It must contain:
	  – a schedule for independent quality assurance reviews of the project, stating who will perform them and at which stages they will be performed
	  – quality goals and objectives
	  – list of anticipated deviations from company policies and standards and approving authority for such deviations
	  – review and approval approach
	  – definition of quality control procedures; the methods, systems, tools, procedures to be adopted to ensure quality is met
	  – software version control and configuration management capability as appropriate
	  – a high level approach to testing, with success criteria defined and descriptions of the more detailed test strategy and procedures that will be developed
	
	• There must be clear accountabilities for each aspect of the QMP and it must be reviewed as required during the project, including at phase transitions and Stage Reviews
		Project manager
		
		Project manager

Table A1.1   continued

Standard	Minimum Requirement	Person Responsible
People management		
People deliver projects, so it is important to structure projects correctly, allocate the right people for the tasks and manage their performance and development As projects are temporary organizations it is also necessary to focus particular attention on team building and on planning for the release and subsequent roles of team members	• Each project role must have clear terms of reference, listing responsibilities, reporting lines, delegated authorities and the competencies required	Accountable executive/project manager
	• At both phase transitions, and at Stage Reviews, the organization structure for the project must be reviewed so that it evolves in line with the needs of each stage	Accountable executive/project manager
	• There must be an assessment of the project-based skills of staff assigned to the project, be they project specialists or BAU staff. This must result in appropriate training and team-building activity	Project manager
	• Succession plans must be in place for key roles on the project. If cover cannot be provided, for reasons of cost or availability, the project manager must note these on the risk register	Project manager
	• Appropriate measures must be in place to ensure that the careers of assigned staff are well managed during their assignment to the project. These must include continuity of service, equity of rewards between the project and BAU roles and inclusion of assigned staff in HR and communications processes within their 'home' department	Project manager
	• Where staff are assigned to a project for more than six months, they must receive a performance appraisal from the project. The PM is required to act as the line manager for this purpose	Project manager
	• Plans must be made for the re-deployment of project staff after the project	Project manager

Table A1.1 *concluded*

Standard	Minimum Requirement	Person Responsible
Procurement Procurement ensures that external suppliers to the organization deliver in line with the overall project goals. This management process starts with the preparation of a contract strategy for the project and continues through a procurement life cycle. Often the project will leave a legacy of contractual relationships for ongoing BAU services	• A contract strategy must be included in the PMP. This strategy must consider the components of the project and assess various options for their supply. It should consider the appropriate use of internal functions, existing suppliers, new contracts, and the use of both consultants and prime contractors/integrators	Project manager
	• The company's procurement and record-keeping procedures must be followed. Where these do not adequately cover project-based purchasing (typically on areas such as delegated authorities), these omissions must be separately agreed and documented so that project progress is not impeded	Project manager
	• The project manager must ensure that appropriate procurement skills are made available to the project. These will range from ad hoc support from a central procurement function, to full-time assignment of a commercial manager	Project manager
	• On major contracts, the organization should expect suppliers to adopt their project management methodology. On smaller contracts, alignment or mapping a supplier's methodology will be adequate	Project manager
	• A contract must be put in place specifying all terms of agreement between the company and supplier. Work in advance of a formal contract will require formal waiver from company procedures	Project manager
	• Where a contract will extend beyond the current stage of the project, this must be made clear, so that the PSC and project investment committee are aware of the nature of the commitment being made	Accountable executive/project manager

Notes on Benefits Management

This appendix provides some notes on the process of managing benefits so as to achieve the agreed business case of the project. Chapter 3 described the critical importance of this process (together with managing the effects of change) and Chapter 4 described how these processes receive even more emphasis in the context of a programme.

These two processes are interdependent:

- benefits cannot be delivered unless some change in the status quo has taken place, while

- change cannot be sustained unless the organization can be convinced that benefits are being delivered (benefits that outweigh the cost and discomfort that change brings).

PROCESS

The process of managing benefits has been mentioned both in Chapter 3 and Appendix 1. This appendix will expand on the process phases and useful techniques.

ANALYSE AND IDENTIFY BENEFITS

Although the strategic benefits of the project will have been established at feasibility stage, this phase of work develops the benefits case in more detail and identifies the desired outcomes or improvement opportunities together with the projects that will deliver them.

DEFINE AND QUANTIFY BENEFITS

A comprehensive register of benefits is developed, each linked to the proposed project investments. Clear linkage is often helped through the use of benefits roadmaps (see later under 'Techniques').

Benefits should be classified into:

- financial

- non-financial but measurable

- intangible.

A customer relationship management (CRM) project was established to allow a bank to improve customer service. It included a range of improvements in how customers were served and the implementation of CRM software to allow the bank to have a single, consolidated view of each customer's relationship with the bank.

Financial benefits:

- improved customer revenues, measured through the number of products that each customer was, on average, purchasing from the bank

- customer assets under management

- reduced overtime

- productivity of call handling.

Non-financial but measurable benefits:

- customer perceptions/satisfaction

- improved customer retention (can be turned into a financial benefit if the link to reduced marketing costs can be shown)

- improved staff satisfaction (often linked closely with improved customer satisfaction and with improved attendance)

- lower staff turnover

- shorter processing times (for example, loan decision times)

- reduced customer waiting times in the call centre.

Intangible benefits:

- flexibility of allocating staff to different roles

- freeing up management time

- reduced paperwork, improving image and professionalism.

An alternative categorization is to assign benefits to the four quadrants of a balanced scorecard, which can be useful if the organization already uses this approach for managing business performance. The categories are:

- financial (for example, revenues, costs)

- customer (customer retention, customer satisfaction, market penetration)

- business process (headcount, processing speed)

- learning (team working, speed of decisions, improved management control).

> Health warning – We should be careful about how benefits are described to stakeholders. People in some organizations react well to the careful analysis of non-financial benefits, whilst others only want to hear about the financial benefits! Consider the audience carefully and focus the messages accordingly.

It might be felt preferable to categorize intangible benefits as 'enablers' in the sense that their real value is that they lead to other, more tangible benefits. Improving the corporate image or responsiveness of the organization are intangible benefits but will lead to other benefits that are more tangible.

OPTIMIZE BENEFITS

This phase seeks to maximize the benefits that can be derived from any specific improvement, then to prioritize improvements in a way that they collectively maximize the benefits to the business. This is key to the sequencing and design of the project or programme.

BASELINE AND DEFINE MEASUREMENT CRITERIA

Having defined the various benefits, a system for measuring progress against a pre-determined baseline needs to be established. Targets for each benefit must be added to the register of benefits established earlier.

Targets must each have a specified time period or date ('reduce customer complaints from a baseline of 50 per week to 25 per week, within four months'). Related factors should be clearly stated ('target is based upon 50 000 customers') so that performance can be compared back to the baseline.

Data capture is key to this phase; in some cases the project will have to build an enhanced management information system to achieve this.

TRACK AND REVIEW BENEFITS REALIZATION

The flow of benefits is monitored using the benefits register. See Chapter 4 for common issues here and Chapter 5 for some solutions. Building financial benefits into BAU budgets is a key way to ensure that they are tracked better by accountable executives.

An occasional formal review should be held to ensure that benefits remain on track or, if not, to agree if the project should be modified.

TECHNIQUES

BENEFITS ROADMAPS

Benefits roadmaps are a way of showing how various benefits are produced by a project or programme. The first version of a roadmap focuses solely on the various outcomes that the project is trying to deliver. Once the team is happy with the logical flow of outcomes, the various projects that deliver these outcomes can be added. It is very important to map the outcomes first, followed by mapping the potential projects. This sequence prompts the project team to consider alternative activities or deliverables that could deliver the same outcome. It also helps the team to appreciate when a given deliverable can deliver multiple benefits.

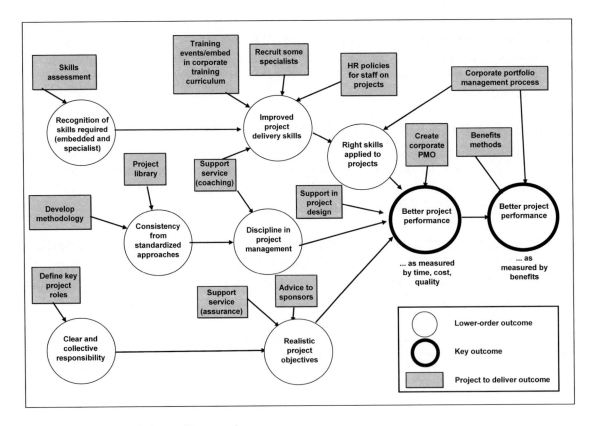

Figure A2.1   A benefits roadmap

As an example, see Figure A2.1. This describes a simple roadmap for a project to improve an organization's project management capability – particularly relevant to this book! Outcomes can be intermediate ('having enough skilled project managers') or final ('better project performance measured by project benefits') and are shown as circles in the figure. Projects are shown as rectangles; some support multiple outcomes.

Some people prefer to map the benefits through a breakdown structure format, although this approach does not illustrate complex dependencies as well as a roadmap.

BENEFITS REGISTER

The benefits register simply lists all agreed benefits, categorized as appropriate and with full detail to allow tracking.

Pay attention to the difference between one-off benefits and recurring benefits, and ensure that recurring costs that result from the project are recognized and subtracted from gross benefits to show the real, net benefit of the project to the organization. The register should show how benefits accrue in a number of years (as benefits usually take some time to achieve a steady state).

The benefits register should also clearly describe who is responsible for the delivery and tracking of each benefit. With a clear description of the benefits and owners, this provides the core of a benefits realization plan that can be included within the project management plan or, if particularly complex, held as a separate project document.

KEY PERFORMANCE INDICATORS

Key performance indicators (KPIs) demonstrate that a change has occurred as targeted by the project. KPIs can be used as leading indicators to demonstrate that progress is being made towards a measurable benefit, even before that eventual benefit is proven. An increase in sales enquiries is a leading indicator that a sales campaign is bearing fruit, even before the campaign results in increased revenues.

We could measure directly the progress made towards a target of increasing the number of a bank's customers who are highly satisfied by levels of service in the branches, but surveys to achieve this are costly and hence used sparingly. Leading indicators can be used in advance, in this case potential indicators being:

- queuing time

- number of closed accounts

- number of customer complaints.

KPIs are particularly useful where an intangible benefit is targeted as they act as a proxy measure to provide some confidence that the desired benefit is going to be achieved.

If we are seeking improved staff morale through a series of changes, then we could use an indicator such as staff turnover to demonstrate that morale was improving.

In summary, where a benefits roadmap establishes the dynamics of cause and effect – explaining which activity will lead to which benefit – the KPIs allow the project team to measure or predict that cause and effect.

OPTIMIZING BENEFITS

Several techniques are available to help optimize how a project (or collection of projects) delivers business benefits:

- Forced pair analysis, which compares each option against every other option in turn, ranking their desirability. This leads to a score for each option, allowing them to be ranked.

- Structured decision-making techniques, scoring each option against a number of criteria to achieve a ranking.

- Grid techniques, where various improvements within the project are plotted to assess their desirability. Typical grids would plot risk against return, cost against return or, at a more holistic level, ease of implementation against attractiveness of the opportunity.

Simple projects will offer limited opportunities to optimize the benefits, either through selecting alternatives or sequencing activities. This concept is of most use in a complex project or a programme (see also Chapter 4). Chapter 5 takes this concept of optimizing activities to a more strategic level, when optimizing activity across all projects in the organization.

SUCCESS FACTORS

With the process and techniques described above we are seeking to comply with the following success factors in realizing business benefits:

- clear accountability for benefits realization;

- accountability that survives past the project implementation and into benefits delivery;

- clear differentiation between the deliverables of a project and its benefits;

- simple techniques to help project teams articulate benefits;

- a strong focus upon financial benefits (for stakeholder engagement), even if other benefits also accrue;

- building management information systems where required to prove a benefit;

- corporate processes to provide governance over the benefits realization of all projects:

— building benefits into future BAU budgets (see Chapter 5);

— using a corporate process for managing project investments to provide oversight of all projects (also Chapter 5).

Notes on Managing Change and Stakeholders

This appendix provides some notes on the process of achieving business acceptance of change. Chapter 3 described the critical importance of this process (together with managing the business case and benefits) and Chapter 4 described how these processes receive even more emphasis in the context of a programme.

We hear much today on the subject of managing change. Some commentators focus on the processes that can be deployed to engage stakeholders and communicate with them, others advocate a programmatic approach so as to aggregate and coordinate change initiatives, whilst others highlight the importance of leadership, concentrating on how a chief executive can mobilize the organization's senior management team to drive a series of changes. Some techniques look at each project as a very discrete exercise in managing change whilst others portray change as a serial activity of corporate renewal, of which projects are merely parts.

Without denigrating any approach, I feel that we often suffer from each of these approaches being presented as the all-purpose answer to managing change – the 'silver bullet' that can be applied universally. The simplistic use of a supposedly universal approach will gloss over the uniqueness of each organization, project and stakeholder. In reality, each project has to address the challenge of change in a very systematic way and from first principles, not simply by applying a generic approach.

Whilst each approach or technique will have its own points of merit, I am also struck that they typically describe the actions and processes that any good project manager should be carrying out:

- considering the effects of the project on the organization;

- ensuring that clear business leadership underpins the project;

- engaging support;

- communicating to affected parties.

PROJECT DESIGN

The project manager's work starts with the design of the project:

- What type of change will my project create?

- What is the climate in the organization – is it ready for the change that my project will create?

- What level of stress, caused by other changes, already exists?

- Who are the key stakeholders and what is unique about the perspectives and needs of each of them?

- How should project work be designed and governed to reflect this?

THE CHANGE STRATEGY

The process of managing change must be guided by a clear strategy. It will be based upon the initial design questions posed above and will shape each unique project in the following ways:

- Ensuring that the criteria by which each stakeholder would judge the success of the project (success that could be defined in organizational or personal terms!) are clear and incorporated in the project's plans.

- Deciding how the project team ensures that each stakeholder supports the project (or at least does not stand in its way):

  - Who needs to be engaged closely and who needs simply to be informed?

  - What is the right balance between directing the change (telling) and engaging stakeholders (selling)?

  - Do we need agents or advocates to help the project's influence spread across the organization?

  - Is there a layer of management who could obstruct the change (some commentators refer to this as a 'permafrost' layer of managers who are cynical about change or whose position is threatened by the change)?

- Considering how change issues will affect the scope of the project (for example, when changing working practices have we also included changes in rewards or other means of reinforcement)?

- Setting the pace of the project and deciding if the project should be a single, 'big bang' event or a series of smaller stages.

- Deciding the sequence of engaging and communicating with various stakeholders.

- Reinforcing the strategy with the appropriate governance processes and bodies.

Based upon this strategy, the process of gaining business acceptance of change continues throughout the life cycle of the project – communicating, engaging, monitoring for changes in business or user needs, maintaining management commitment, and building a structured approach to acceptance of the project's solution into operation. This will require leadership from the project manager and, even more critically, the accountable executive and sponsor. It will also require the allocation of adequate resource and budget (and without the project manager forcing these 'soft' considerations into the project's budget, they will get excluded).

TECHNIQUES

The first technique of note, particularly useful in more complex or enterprise-wide projects, is to carefully map out all of the stakeholders to the project. Figure A3.1 shows one approach.

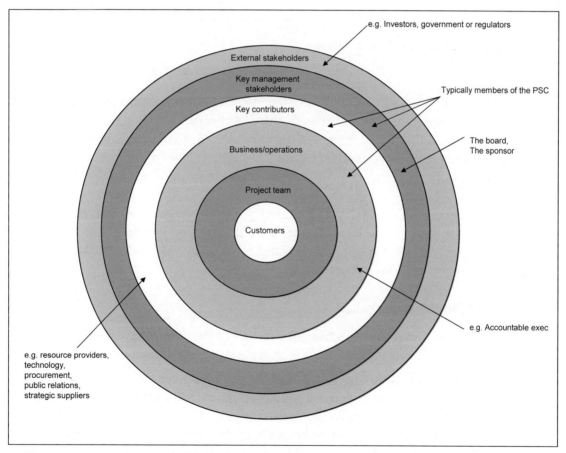

Figure A3.1   Identifying all stakeholders

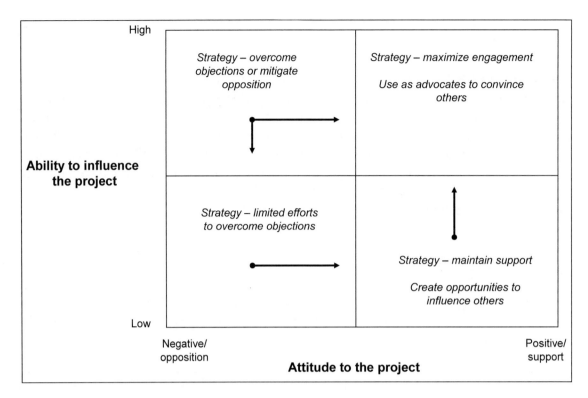

Figure A3.2   Stakeholder analysis

Having identified all stakeholders, the most common technique used to help project teams think carefully about the attitudes of the various stakeholders is to map their potential interaction with the project through some form of grid. Figure A3.2 shows one version, which aims to assess their influence and their level of support or opposition to the project and then identify appropriate strategies to interact with stakeholders.

In a complex organization some people will oppose a project. Too often, commentary on managing change assumes that objectors are motivated by personal opinion or other unacceptable reasons, but this opposition could be for very valid reasons, so the role of the project manager includes being the conscience for the organization:

- Are the objections valid?

- Should we alter the objectives or solution of the project as a result?

Health warning – Given the importance of managing stakeholders, it is tempting for any project manager to document the approach clearly using these techniques and apply it openly (as most advisors on the subject would recommend). However, this will not always work in practice because of the essentially political nature of any organization. Much of the analysis and application of these techniques has to be kept closed and applied with great caution. The sponsor and accountable executive must play their part. The project manager must learn to be comfortable with some key aspects of the project remaining undocumented and managed informally!

SUCCESS FACTORS

With the process and techniques described above, we are seeking to comply with the following success factors to manage change through stakeholders:

- Be clear on the changes required and how they link to a business goal, stressing benefits not project features (for otherwise you will never engage senior executives).

- Recognize that each stakeholder has a unique view of the benefits of the project and its success criteria. Pay particular attention to middle management layers.

- Communicate clearly and often – make it two-way and be regarded as the monopoly supplier of good information about the project.

- Have either a champion with influence or a number of agents of change.

- Remember that acceptance is a process that operates throughout the life cycle (building engagement and ownership takes time – acceptance is not simply a phase at the end of the life cycle!).

- Create discomfort with the existing situation, but prepare staff so that you reduce the discomfort of change.

- Recognize that stakeholders' attitudes and the appropriate change management strategy will change as the project progresses.

- Don't ignore resistance – at a minimum manage it, ideally convert into support.

- Use supporters to convert others.

- Set short-term goals and a pace of work that creates a sense of urgency.

- Processes and IT systems alone do not alter behaviour – remember to include reward systems and organizational structures, policies, delegated powers, symbols of change (and of course leadership) as levers to promote or reinforce changes in behaviour.

Notes on Risk Assessment

Risk assessment is a critical aspect of the management of every project. As a project becomes more risky, the management approach becomes more sophisticated, the processes that are used to control the project must become more robust and the needs for experienced staff, executive governance and independent assurance all increase.

The use of risk assessment also ensures that we do not burden every project with high levels of control that are only warranted for the most risky of initiatives; hence we can avoid the danger of bureaucracy for its own sake.

This appendix outlines a typical way in which the level of project risk can be classified and how the classification is used to guide the control framework that should deliver a successful project.

RISK CLASSIFICATION

Risk classification rates a project according to the perceived risks. There are three risk classes:

- high risk

- medium risk

- low risk.

It might be useful to add a further classification of 'critical project' to highlight those projects where success is particularly important to the organization's performance and they therefore require particular attention at executive levels. A project could be classified as critical when it meets one or more of the following criteria:

- Project costs are greater than a given amount (which will be a significant impact upon the organization's cost base).

- The project is strategically important to the organization, which might include projects where:

- — there will be a significant direct impact on the market reputation of the organization;

- — a long-term partnership is being embarked upon with a strategic supplier (for example, outsourcing);

- — the project is a pilot for a larger, more far-reaching programme; or

- — the project incorporates complex new technology or will result in new ways of doing business, across a broad part of the organization.

For simplicity, the following examples are limited to assessing low, medium and high risk projects.

PROCEDURE

To determine the risk classification, a project is assessed against five risk categories:

1. Size and timescale

2. Complexity

3. Experience

4. Commercial risk

5. Business impact.

Note how the focus on the risks of delivering the solution (related to size, complexity and experience) which make up the traditional focus of risk analysis in 'hard' projects is balanced by considering the business impact and risks to commercial success of the project.

These risk categories are further subdivided into specific risk factors. Within each risk factor there are three possible risk scores – 1, 2 or 3. The scores awarded for each factor are averaged to achieve an overall risk rating for the project. To carry out risk classification:

1. Score each risk factor using the risk ratings indicated in Table A4.1.

2. Add the scores for each of the five risk categories and calculate the average risk rating for each category.

3. Total the ratings to give a maximum project score of 15.

4. Classify the risk according to total score as follows: Low: less than 7; Medium: 7 to 11; High: 12 to 15.

Table A4.1   Risk classification of projects

Risk category	Risk factor	1	2	3
Project size and timescale	Cost	< £1 m	< £2 m	> =£2 m
	Project duration (including feasibility)	< 3 months	< 9 months	> =9 months
	Achievability of timescale	Confident in both timescale and likely level of contingency	Demanding – timescale may have insufficient contingency	Very demanding – timescale is very tight and has no contingency
	End date	Not imposed	Imposed internally	Imposed externally
Complexity	Project objectives	Detailed scope clearly understood and agreed	High-level scope understood and agreed	Scope not yet agreed
	Business areas impacted	Single business unit and single geography	Multiple business units or multiple geography	Multiple business units and multiple geography
	External parties	No external supplier involved	1 external supplier involved	Significant involvement of > 1 external supplier
	Degree of change	No operational change	Minor operational changes	Major operational changes
	Dependence on other projects	Single, self-contained project	Dependence to/from one project	Dependence to/from multiple projects
Experience	Organizational experience	Done before	1st time in business unit or geography	1st time in organization
	Team experience	Project management and team skills available within business unit or geography	Project management and team skills available in group (but not in business unit or geography)	Project management and team skills in scarce supply
	Technology risk	Familiar technology	Technology new to business unit or geography	Technology new to organization
Commercial risk	Business risk	Familiar business process/product	Business process/product new to business unit or geography	Business process/product new to organization
	Market risk	Expansion within existing market	New product provided to existing market or existing product provided to new market	New product in a new market

continued

	Stability of local environment in which the project is operating	Stable	Moderate degree of instability	Unstable
Risk category	*Risk factor*	*1*	*2*	*3*
	Competition	Limited	Moderate, some competitor reaction to the project	Dynamic, project will lead to significant responses from competitors
	Effect (+ or –) on reputation	Minimal	Moderate	Significant
Business impact	Impact on annual results – results affected by:	< 0.1%	< 0.5%	> =0.5%
	Strategic significance	Minimal	Moderate	Significant
	Customer impact	Minimal	Moderate	Significant
	Regulatory impact	Minimal	Some negotiations required with one or more regulators	Significant negotiations with one or more regulators
	Market impact	No + or – impact on share price	Moderate + or – impact on share price	Significant + or – impact on share price

Numbers are illustrative; they will vary by organization to reflect whatever costs and business impacts are deemed material to the organization.

This approach to assessing risk is intentionally quite simple, but structured and reasonably objective. It can be tailored depending upon the nature of the organization. For example, an organization operating in very volatile markets might want to emphasize the risks that impact upon the commercial success of the project, whereas an organization with numerous logistically challenging projects might wish to emphasize the risks of complexity and timescale.

Table A4.2 provides a worked example. Each risk factor is scored, then an average calculated for each of the five risk categories. These five are added to provide a total score for the project. The project in this worked example is of average size and complexity for the organization, but has some elevated risk of solution delivery because of a shortage of project management skills, the presence of new technology and multiple external suppliers. Commercial risk is average, although a strong response is expected from the competition.

When rating project size, it is important that the total scope of work is used. For example, a preliminary study that is intended to lead to a much larger project should be classified according to its likely eventual size. The project team might not like the added attention to their fledgling project, but the organization must ensure that the objectives and design of the project are shaped correctly and in recognition of its eventual impact.

Table A4.2   **Worked example of risk assessment**

Risk category	Risk factor	Notes	Score	Category total	Rounded average
Project size and timescale	Cost	Preliminary estimate £1.5 m	2		
	Project duration (incl. feasibility)	7 months	2		
	Achievability of timescale	Confident	1		
	End-date	To be agreed	1	6	1.5
Complexity	Project objectives	Clear, agreed statement of objectives	1		
	Business areas impacted	Single business unit	1		
	External parties	Software supplier, external systems integrator	3		
	Degree of change	Some operational impact	2		
	Dependence to/from other projects	None	1	8	1.6
Experience	Organizational experience	Similar project elsewhere in group	2		
	Team experience	Project management skills in scarce supply	3		
	Technology risk	Technology new to business unit	3	8	2.7
Commercial risk	Business risk	Change to business processes	2		
	Market risk	New product to existing market	2		
	Stability of local environment in which the project is operating	Stable	1		
	Competition	Strong response from competitors	3		
	Reputation	Medium	2	10	2.0
Business impact	Impact on annual results	< 0.2%	2		
	Strategic significance	Potential strategic significance	2		
	Customer impact	Potential impact on local customer base through improved service levels	2		
	Regulatory impact	None	1		
	Market impact	Medium	2	9	1.8
TOTAL					**9.6**

With a score of 9.6, the project is medium-risk.

The assessment of risk can be refined as more information is gained or there are changes to the environment within which the project is delivered, for example if market stability or competition changes.

The accountable executive is responsible for carrying out the project risk classification using the procedure outlined below and must encourage the participation of all interested parties, including where necessary appropriate experts. The assessment must take place early in the feasibility phase of a project.

During the detailed planning phase, the project manager must undertake a more thorough assessment of these risk categories, coupled with identification of mitigating actions and contingency plans. The assessment must be documented and the details included in the project management plan and project request.

USING RISK CLASSIFICATION

Note that, with just this relatively simple assessment of risk in Table A4.2, we can identify some important characteristics of the selected project that lead to elevated levels of risk. From these observations, we can consider mitigating actions within the project design. Given the risks stated above, this risk mitigation embedded into the project design could include, in this case:

- ensuring technology participation on the project steering committee;
- a dedicated and experienced resource for supplier management;
- recruiting external project management skills (or perhaps some coaching service);
- close linkages with business managers to ensure that any change in direction required by competitive pressures can be made in a timely manner.

In addition to helping in project design, the risk assessment has a more formal role. It is used to set out the level of governance and assurance that is appropriate to its risk. In particular, the accountable executive and project manager should use risk classification to help define the following:

- appropriate approval mechanisms
- level of progress reporting required
- level of project management experience needed to run the project
- nature and formality of external reviews
- level of audit involvement required.

Table A4.3 shows a typical way in which this control framework is adjusted to reflect the classifications of high, medium and low risk projects.

Table A4.3   **Using risk classification to set out the control framework for the project**

	Low risk	*Medium risk*	*High risk*
Project approval required	If less than £1m – Project Request (PR) only, produced at the end of detailed planning stage If more than £1m, Concept Paper produced at early stage and Project Request produced at the end of feasibility stage and/or at the end of detailed planning		Concept Paper produced at early stage and Project Request produced at the end of feasibility stage and/or at the end of detailed planning Approval by member of board (or full board depending on project cost) Subject to review by project investment committee
Independent review of Project Request	If project value is >£1m the Project Request must be reviewed independently to assess project risk and establish project design Project investment committee review of project design is optional and focused on capabilities/skills of the core project team		All Project Requests reviewed independently to assess project risk and establish project design. Input from senior peers or external consultants Full review of project design (includes stakeholders and change management) by project investment committee
Group reporting	Quarterly report submitted to PMO in the business unit but can be aggregated with other projects for reporting to the corporate PMO	Quarterly project scorecard to be submitted for each project and copied to corporate PMO	
Level of project management experience	Project manager	Senior project manager	Senior project manager or project director
Governance	Project steering committee. Sponsor can also be accountable executive	Separate project steering committee and project working committee are mandatory. Separate sponsor and accountable executive are mandatory	
Healthcheck reviews to be undertaken	Peer review inside project team	Peer review inside project team, supplemented by business unit review	Peer review inside project team, business unit review and occasional non-business unit review, for example by the corporate PMO or an external consultant
Audit involvement	Internal audit alerted to project, at the discretion of the accountable executive. Progress reports forwarded if requested by audit	Internal audit alerted to project during detailed planning, before Project Request sign-off. Progress reports issued to audit thereafter	Internal audit alerted to project during feasibility. Progress reports issued to audit thereafter. Audit represented on the project steering committee, at their discretion. Detailed audit work may be undertaken at key milestones

Costs are illustrative; they will vary by organization to reflect whatever is defined as material worth and impact to the organization.

Inspection of Table A4.3 shows the close linkage between risk assessment and the careful design of the project – reiterating why both techniques are included within the process for 'Project initiation, planning and staging' as described in Appendix 1. This relationship between risk and design of the project is, as mentioned in Chapter 3, rarely articulated in BAU organizations and a key area for improved project performance.

Notes on the Use of Stages in Projects

WHY STAGE PROJECTS?

Significant projects should be delivered as stages. The objectives of this are to:

- manage risk by releasing funding progressively;

- improve our ability to swiftly adjust investment between projects as market conditions change;

- encourage the regular search for new benefits opportunities that the project can address;

- reduce payback periods by seeking phased delivery of benefits;

- ensure that, if we terminate a project in favour of more attractive opportunities, we have gained some lasting benefit from the work already completed.

WHICH PROJECTS DO WE STAGE?

Typically, the following types of project would be staged:

- any project where its size and duration make it material to an organization's resources and performance. Typically this would be projects with implementation periods of more than 1 to 1.5 years;

- any project that requires non-BAU funding for a discrete design/build phase before the full implementation can be estimated. Examples would be:

  — a major platform investment, where the first stage might be a significant detailed planning process including prototyping technologies and new processes;

  — an initiative in a new area, where preliminary research is needed to determine project scope;

  — the development of a standard design to underpin an organization-wide project.

HOW TO USE STAGES ON PROJECTS

The guiding principle is that each stage should deliver tangible benefits. It is recognized that some projects might require more than one stage before benefits start to flow, so these will need approval as exceptions and in these exceptional cases project teams should also investigate alternative approaches that accelerate the delivery of benefits.

Projects can be staged in three main ways:

- by implementing the scope or functionality in stages;

- by implementing global projects progressively across countries rather than in one stage;

- by implementing projects progressively across business units rather than across the entire business in one stage.

IMPLEMENTING THE SCOPE/FUNCTIONALITY IN STAGES

Where the scope of the project can be broken down by functionality, for example when the solution is based upon modular technologies, this offers a straightforward way of using project stages. Packaged business applications for manufacturing, logistics, human resources or financial control are typical candidates. In the latter, one can implement the general ledger functionality within the application but defer other modules, perhaps accounts payable or fixed assets. This not only phases the delivery of the technology part of the solution but also allows the associated process changes to be phased, reducing risk and complexity.

On some projects, initial benefits can be gained by identifying relatively simple, operational changes (which usually means that they do not require complex technology solutions). Customer relationship management projects can implement some simple ways of improving workflow in the customer-facing departments as a first stage (for example, by providing easier access to documents) before starting the complex and expensive work to implement the software application for customer relationship management.

Even within a specific area of functionality, there can be opportunities to stage the implementation. It is generally accepted that most technology solutions are over-specified by users, and project teams should look for the core deliverables that generate most business value. This logic is used by rapid application development methods, which stage deliverables by categories such as:

- must have now

- should have now

- could have now

- will not do until later.

IMPLEMENTING PROGRESSIVELY ACROSS COUNTRIES

This approach simply stages the project by country. This allows the project team to prioritize activity:

- implementing first where the highest benefits are available; or

- implementing first where the risks are lowest; or

- in practice, some blend of the two that optimizes risk and return.

This approach applies particularly to projects implemented by country-organized functions. The roll-out of new human resources processes and the market launches of retail banking products in banking are examples. Each of these is likely to be based upon a standard, core offering but must be tailored in each country to suit regulations, market needs and working practices. Prioritizing activity by countries allows us to schedule the tailoring efficiently and optimize risk and return across the project.

This approach also applies to regulatory projects, where the dates for compliance and the detailed requirements will vary by country.

IMPLEMENTING PROGRESSIVELY ACROSS BUSINESSES

This approach is relevant for projects that have an impact across the organization, but do not have to be implemented at the same time by every business unit. These could be functional processes such as human resources processes (as listed above; we can stage these by business or country) or business efficiency projects such as outsourcing or the use of shared service centres (where we can choose the priority that delivers the best return on investment).

Good central control is required to ensure that the nature of the solution does not change (except where beneficial) as it is rolled out to each business area.

OTHER BENEFITS

Whichever approach is used, there are some additional benefits including the opportunity to learn from the initial stages, developing a template for the project approach and using this to improve the delivery of later stages. Some projects maximize this learning by using the 'tiger team' approach of a central team actively driving each stage, one after the other.

A staged approach can also be used to assess the capability of a vendor before full commitment is made, if there are perceived risks or 'leading edge' solutions.

ISSUES THAT RESULT

There are some issues that result from staging projects:

- *Timescales* – having a single, discrete pilot stage will usually reduce overall project duration by reducing risk and rework. But as more stages are used, the overall timescales will inevitably extend, as will the final delivery of all benefits.

- *Costs*

  - Up-front costs – depending upon the commercial structure, the project might need to pre-invest in solutions that will only be partially used in the first project stage (for example, global software licences).

  - Support costs – if the project is replacing an existing capability, the use of stages can extend the period of parallel operation of new and old solutions and this increases costs. This is exacerbated by possible inconsistencies in solution and business practices between the various stages (for example, vendor software might be upgraded between stages).

- *Global designs* – where the project is staged by country or business, some form of global design is critical to achieving consistency between the stages. Stakeholders for future stages need to provide input to the project early on, through the governance process and by participating in the design team, even though their implementation is not planned until much later. There is an opportunity cost in the use of these scarce resources well ahead of implementation.

Index